TIME MANAGE YOUR READING

To my husband Raymond, with thanks for his help in writing this book, and with all my love.

Time Manage your Reading

Shirley Rudd

Gower

Published by
Gower Publishing Company Limited
Gower House
Croft Road
Aldershot
Hants GU11 3HR
England

British Library Cataloguing in Publication Data

Rudd, Shirley
  Time Manage your Reading
  1. Reading Skills. Self-development – Manuals
  I. Title
  428.4'3

  ISBN 0 566 02762 3

Printed and bound in Great Britain by
Biddles Ltd, Guildford and King's Lynn

Contents

Preface

The demands made on executives today are formidable. One of their most difficult tasks is to keep up to date with not only the technical aspects of their jobs but also the economic, political and social environment in which they operate. To do this they are forced to spend an enormous amount of time reading, and yet the reading skills they use have probably been neglected since the age of about eight.

The main objective of this book is to help executives to increase both their reading efficiency and the satisfaction they derive from the process. The confidence that they can cope will in itself lead to a reduction in tension. A further objective is to show that improved reading can produce excitement and creativity.

Unlike most of the existing books on reading skills, this one is designed explicitly for executives. Of course it would be equally useful to members of the professions and indeed anyone seeking more effective methods of dealing with printed material.

The text is arranged in a logical step-by-step sequence. I have chosen a dialogue form of presentation which will enable readers to identify with 'Digby Porter' as he builds up a repertoire of reading skills under the guidance of his boss and mentor 'James Harrington'. One of the advantages of this treatment is that it offers immediate answers to questions likely to occur to readers.

Reading should be an enjoyable experience and I hope that this book will entertain as well as instruct.

Shirley Rudd

Acknowledgements

I should like to acknowledge the sources I have used to illustrate the text. Each is identified by a footnote within the book.

'Facing the fax', *Business*, January 1987.
Queen Victoria and the Bonapartes, Theo Aronson, Macmillan, New York.
The Skills of Training, Leslie Rae, Gower, Aldershot, 1983.
'What to do when you're feeling blue', *Working Woman*, November, 1985 (no longer in print).
The World Book Encyclopedia, World Book, Inc., Chicago.

My thanks, also, to Stephen Ashton, Science/Maths Publishing Director for Heinemann Educational Books who provided two of the diagrams in Chapter 11: 'Computer studies for GCSE' and 'Science module for mixed abilities of pupils'.

SR

1 Reading for meaning

James Harrington's office, late one Wednesday afternoon.

James Harrington – Managing Director
Digby Porter – one of his executives

JAMES: 'I see you haven't got through all that bumf yet and I gave it to you weeks ago.'

DIGBY: 'I just haven't had time to read it all – so many articles, reports, marked chapters in journals and. . .'

JAMES: 'But you're one of my most competent people. You time-manage your activities so well.'

DIGBY: 'Well I don't seem to be able to do it with my reading. There are hundreds of thousands of words you've handed me to go through. If I were to read every page you've set me, reading all day and all weekend, it would take me two months, let alone two weeks. And that's without doing any other work.'

JAMES: 'Sit down, Digby. Now obviously I didn't intend you to read hundreds of thousands of words.'

DIGBY: 'Then how do I take in the information?'

JAMES: 'By reading the passage for meaning, for what it says, not every word, phrase, sentence.'

DIGBY: 'Of course I'm reading for meaning.'

JAMES: 'You're not really. You're reading words.'

DIGBY: 'Huh?'

JAMES: 'Just relate the subject to art for a moment. Do you know Van Gogh's "Sunflowers" – the one in the National Gallery?'

DIGBY: 'Very well.'

JAMES: 'How many sunflowers are there in the painting?'

DIGBY: 'I haven't a clue.'

JAMES: 'What colour are most of the flowers?'

DIGBY: 'Yellow.'

JAMES: 'Wrong Digby, orange. The background is bright yellow which gives it the feeling of yellow. You didn't need to see the details, how he constructed his painting in order to sense the message of the golden sunflowers. You looked at the picture as a whole. Van Gogh used his paint exuberantly to convey his own excitement and you got caught up in its emotional power. Right? You didn't stare at every brushstroke, analyse how he placed his yellow strokes next to his orange next to his greens and why. You didn't need to count the number of flowers to "feel" and to "experience" them.

Reading is the same. Think about it. Just what are you trying to achieve by reading every word, devouring every detail of the reading material I gave you? You're not supposed to learn it by heart.'

DIGBY: 'But if the writer never meant me to read every word, why did he write them?'

JAMES: 'Words are the writer's tools, as paint is the artist's. The artist uses paint to tell you something, the writer uses words. The writer has his thought, a single unit, which he expresses in a line or lines of words. You, the reader, must then reconstruct the words into the original thought of the writer. Stop thinking of a page of print as a collection of words. It is technically, of course, but you must ignore that. You must think of it as telling you something, giving you a message. It's alive with *story, events, activities, people, feelings, thoughts, ideas, atmosphere, colour, movement.* Even the most technical non-fiction is concerned with putting across an idea, a message, an instruction, a method and so on.'

DIGBY: 'I've never thought of it that way before.'

JAMES: 'That's because when you first learned to read you learned about words and more words and have never been taught to regard them as the nuts and bolts of the information they're imparting. Bricks and cement, nails and screws lying on a pavement bear little resemblance to the house they'll finally become when put together. And when you look at the house, you don't look at those components individually, you "experience" the whole entity. Words on their own are meaningless. Think of a vocabulary list, it tells you nothing. Similarly you don't analyse every mouthful of a delicious gateau – how many eggs were used or quantities of flour and butter. It would ruin the taste.

In reading, if you worry about the words making up the meaning, you lose their power. Only when the words are put together in meaningful units do they serve a purpose. And, what's more, only about 50 per cent of words carry any real meaning; the rest serve them, join them, hold them in place if you like. Just like gelatine in a pudding.

Reading is a mental process. The mind must dictate the amount of print it can understand at any one time.

So, read everything as fast as your mind needs you to, to get the message it sets out to give you. Don't let your eyes slow you down by devouring every word.

Let's do a quick exercise. I'll give you a split second to read what's on this piece of paper. [Holds up paper briefly.] What have I written?'

```
┌─────────────────┐
│   The cat sat   │
│     on the      │
│     the mat     │
└─────────────────┘
```

DIGBY: 'The cat sat on the mat.'
JAMES: 'Read it slowly this time.'
[Digby does so.]
DIGBY: 'I saw only one "the".'
JAMES: 'So you should. Any reasonably competent reader would read that whole familiar phrase in one fixation, one glance, take in its meaning, and not notice the extra "the". By looking at the whole phrase as a single unit, using a wide peripheral vision, that is, a horizontal and vertical one, you

received the message through the few key words, disregarding the rest. The mature reader mentally ignores the words, and is only concerned with the meaning they impart.

Man thinks in terms of wholes, of meaning units – Gestalts, as the psychologists would say. Take the following statement:

The dog bit the boy.

What do you see? Presumably, not a dog, a boy and a bite in the middle. Right?'

DIGBY: 'Right.'

JAMES: 'Similarly, if I say:

The huge black dog bit the small scrawny boy.

you see just that one unpleasant scene unfolding before you. In this case, of course, you heard it from my spoken words which produced a single entity, a picture, a story as your mind sees it.

In the same way – I can't stress it enough – in reading it is the ideas that one needs, the picture being conveyed by the words, the content of them. By "soft-focusing" on the words, you can forget them individually and concentrate on the thought they convey. See what I mean?'

DIGBY: 'I think so.'

JAMES: 'Now read this paragraph I'm scribbling for you. Read it right through.'

sense jumbled no make when fluently words read are to possible not is but feel how much faster you can now go when you can take up the meaning of what you are reading.

DIGBY: 'I do see what you mean. Though I still don't see how that's going to help me get through all those articles.'

JAMES: 'It won't on its own of course, but it's a start. If you want to time-manage your reading, cope with all the mass of work-related print you need to get through, you have to be efficient, which means simply *achieve the best results with a minimum waste of time and energy.* And that involves learning a whole range of new skills.'

DIGBY: 'Skills?'

JAMES: 'Yes, skills. Reading is a highly complicated process which relies on a great variety of skills, and skills is the operative word here. Everyone can improve their skills in reading as they can their golf or tennis, with correct guidance. Just think about this. Reading is vital to daily life. Not a day goes past without reading, even if it's only selecting the correct cereal packet from the kitchen shelf or reading a street sign. Yet from about the age of eight, when most children master the basic skills in reading, they never learn to read again – excluding of course those with remedial problems, but we're not discussing that. Schools don't equip their pupils very well for reading demands made on them in later years at school and certainly not after school. Parents don't hesitate to provide coaching for their children in fields such as maths, French, or sporting activities, but amazingly their reading is ignored.'

DIGBY: 'True. But I must say, it would never occur to me that my kids might need extra reading lessons. After all, they did learn to read and they do pretty well in school from what I can see. In fact, why should they need extra coaching in reading if they're coping well right now?'

JAMES: 'They probably don't need it at this moment, they're still young. But when they're adults I'll bet they do, for over the years bad habits develop in everyone's reading and nothing is ever done to eliminate them. Have you had any reading lessons since you were a child?'

DIGBY: 'Definitely not.'

JAMES: 'Consider sport again. Bjorn Borg, champion among champions, had his coach constantly at his side, monitoring and correcting the tiny faults in his play. No one monitors our reading or keeps an eye on any bad habits we may develop over the years in our silent reading which is largely neglected in schools.'

DIGBY: 'That's a good point.'

JAMES: 'What's more, we never learn to cope with the great variety of reading situations that come into our lives as we develop. Everything a child of eight or nine reads after all is more or less in the same format. Now, as an adult, an executive like yourself will cover a diversity of different reading materials such as journals, memos, letters, newspapers. . .'

DIGBY: 'Advertising literature, documents. . .'

JAMES: 'Not forgetting general magazines, light novels, serious works and so on. And no doubt you attack them all in the same way as you did when you were ten. It would be like Borg approaching every opponent in the same way, using the same court-craft, or rather *no* courtcraft, for any of them.

The point I'm trying to make is that you, together with other literate adults today, have mastered only the basic skills in reading and it's not surprising you're so inefficient and find it all impossible to cope with. You're swamped in a sea of print. There are probably four times as many books on any one subject today as there were thirty years ago. Improved education, the knowledge explosion and the paperback are responsible for that.

So it's become even more important for a reader to firstly, select ruthlessly what to read, and secondly, to read what he or she does select, more efficiently.'

DIGBY: 'What you say makes sense, but what do I do about it? I can't develop my reading all over again and I still have to get through all that junk – sorry, I mean. . .'

JAMES: 'Junk a lot of it may well be. It's for you to sift out what is and discard it, without wasting time reading it all. In other words you need to acquire better reading skills aimed at perfecting the ratio between expended effort and useful work.'

DIGBY: 'As I say, how do I acquire those skills now?'

JAMES: 'With my guidance and tuition.'

DIGBY: 'It's very kind of you, James, to waste your valuable time on me.'

JAMES: 'I'm no philanthropist. All my executives could do with time-management reading skills if they're to get through their work-related reading material efficiently. And to begin with that involves more advanced reading skills.

At a rough guess I'd say the average executive spends at least 15 per cent of his time on direct work-related reading, plus all the newspaper and outside reading he needs to give him a well-rounded background in his field. Not to mention what he can gain from worthwhile fiction and broader reading generally.

As Sir Francis Bacon put it, "reading maketh a full man". But for the moment, I'll be content with the "full" executive on the job.

Fortunately we have a few months to work on this now as the XX project involving all this reading has been postponed.'

DIGBY: 'What a relief. So where do I go from here?'

JAMES: 'You start at the beginning. Step one, go home tonight, find yourself a novel. . .'

DIGBY: 'A novel?'

JAMES: 'Yes, a novel, and what's more a relatively simple and straightforward one. Forget your work load for the moment. You want to start learning new skills on simple material. You wouldn't learn to ski on the difficult slopes, would you? You'd begin with the nursery ones. Narrative is the easiest form of reading so begin there. Start reading the novel, get through a couple of chapters concentrating only on reading for meaning. Don't muddle the word with the thing. "If you hold and fondle each word," as Korzybski, the father of semantics claims, "you're fondling the empty shell when the valuable part is gone." Pretend you're watching a film if it helps and read it for the action. What's bothering you now?'

DIGBY: 'Well, James, I hope I can manage a few chapters tonight. I'll be home late and by the time I get to bed, my eyes never stay open reading.'

JAMES: 'That doesn't surprise me, for two reasons. Firstly, I'm quite sure you must be boring yourself to death reading too slowly, and that will certainly put you to sleep. The brain is capable of taking in ideas at thousands of words a minute and reading at the slow rate I'm quite sure you do, like most people, *must* put your brain to sleep. Especially as it is a bright brain I have to admit, apart from its reading methods. It's like watching an entire movie in slow motion or listening to some plodding bore being interviewed on television. If they'd only speed up, even if what they said was nonsense the pace alone would keep one's attention. I doubt if there's ever been an orator worthy of that name who spoke too slowly.

It's the same with reading. Automatically reading for every detail, word or phrase, becomes as boring and wasteful of time and energy as chewing a piece of boiled fish with the same thoroughness as a piece of steak. And, I'm sure you'll agree, few can afford to waste time these days, least of all in this organization.'

DIGBY: 'How do you define a slow reader?'

JAMES: 'There is no single rate one can read everything, but it has been calculated that the average reader, like yourself I suppose, with reasonably straightforward material, reads at about 250 words per minute and sometimes less. Frankly, that's probably over generous.'

DIGBY: 'What makes you say that?'

JAMES: 'I have a habit when I'm not reading myself on trains, aeroplanes or even the underground, of testing other readers around me. I use my stopwatch at times, though mostly I can now time in seconds without it. I know the average words per page of the sort of book someone is reading, and I can see just how long it takes them to read it before moving across to the next. Much closer to 200 words per minute and less even on the simplest book.'

DIGBY: 'And how fast should one read?'

JAMES: 'That depends on dozens of things; we'll come to that later. But on the whole you should be able to read at least twice as fast as your present speed considering you have not worked on your reading skills since childhood. Reading should be one of the fastest forms of communication, twice that of speaking at least.'

DIGBY: 'And it isn't, I take it.'

JAMES: 'No. We tend to speak and read at about the same speed, between 200–300 words per minute.

DIGBY: 'And we should read about twice the speed we speak?'

JAMES: 'Yes. It's ridiculous speaking and reading silently at the same rate. Again, we do this by acquiring bad habits, and lacking know-how. If you could double your speed on average in reading, fitting twelve hours reading into six, well, the rewards would be obvious. But it's not just a question of speeding up, there's far more to it. In fact that's why I dislike the term "speed reading". Reading is a mental process; speed for speed's sake is ridiculous. A college lecturer who did some research on a large group of students found that on average those of them who had attended "speed reading" courses and were reading above 600 words per minute, were not comprehending as well as they should have been. Mind you, he also found that those reading below 300 words per minute gained the worst results in the comprehension tests. As I've said, they bored their brains, lost concentration, missed the wood for the trees. It's – as – if – I – were – to – speak – like – this, saying each word separately, precisely and slowly. The best results were those reading between 300 and 600 words per minute.'

DIGBY: 'What you say is very interesting. You mentioned that there were two reasons I must be finding it difficult to keep my eyes open reading at night. What's the second, apart from boring myself?'

JAMES: 'Simply that reading only strains the eyes if you read word-for-word. Reading for meaning places far less strain on the eyes.'

DIGBY: 'Why?'

JAMES: 'Because zooming in on practically every word or short phrase places more strain on the eye muscles than soft focusing – getting the meaning from them en masse as it were. It's like wearing blinkers, or trying to examine the works inside a tiny wristwatch without a magnifying glass – the eyes strain through over focusing. Imagine walking into a room and staring at each and every individual item in it. It's more strain than looking around at the general effect. Just to emphasize my point, it's like picking up peanut by peanut from a split packet rather than in handfuls, far more strain on the fingers, not to mention wasting time and energy.'

DIGBY: 'Right, well I'll see what I can do. But one last thing – how will I be able to tell if I'm improving?'

JAMES: 'You'll feel it, you'll feel it. But if you're so keen to map your progress, I'll show you how to calculate your speed per minute. Of course you should have tested yourself before having had even this one little lesson, because I'm sure you'd have found there was already a difference, but it's not too late. I'll send a sheet around to your office of how to calculate your progress. (Readers who wish to do this should turn to the Appendix, page 173.)

Before you go, let's clarify your objectives over the next few weeks:

1   The basic objective is to learn to time-manage your reading so that you can get through it all without wasting time and energy.
2   To improve the quality of your reading.
3   To feel no tension over it.
4   To get more pleasure from all your reading.

We'll make this a weekly session, Wednesdays 5.30. Be here next Wednesday, and let me know how you're getting along. You're bound to have a dozen questions to ask. We'll go from there.'

DIGBY: 'Thanks James, I'll do my best.'

JAMES: 'And remember, take an ordinary run-of-the-mill novelist, not Tolstoy; perhaps a Jeffrey Archer or some other best seller. And make a list of all those things you're reading for: you know, story, colour, movement, ideas and so on. Look through it every time before you read till it's firmly registered in that head of yours and becomes an automatic part of your "think-read". Remember, reading is a mental process. You just happen to use your eyes for it.'

DIGBY: 'Will do. Thanks, see you Wednesday.'

Summary

Reading is a skill. All skills can be improved with guidance.

Read for meaning. Forget about individual words, read what the words tell you.

Reading is a mental process. Your 'mind' should dictate how fast you go, not your eyes.

Executive action

Find a simple novel and read as much as you can, reading for meaning. That is, read for the story, the events, the message, the ideas, the thoughts, the colour, the feelings.

Try this also with any simple work-related reading material. Remember that when learning new skills, it is easiest on simple material.

2 Overcoming guilt

JAMES: 'Guilty?'

DIGBY: 'Yes, I feel guilty now. I'm going faster but I feel I'm missing a lot.'

JAMES: 'Actually I expected that reaction. From the first day you learnt to read you were told to read every word and like a conscientious pupil you did just that. Now you find the habit difficult to break, but there's no need to feel that way. Take walking into a room. Do you notice everything about it, every chair, every painting, every ornament?'

DIGBY: 'No.'

JAMES: 'Precisely. You don't need to take note of every detail unless you're setting out to redecorate the place. You get the feel of it, register the main features that'll tell you the "story" about the room. It wouldn't matter if there were four, five or even six lamps in the room and you hadn't noticed more than three, so long as you were aware of the lighting and the general atmosphere that it gives a room. But even if you had noticed all, the chances are that you wouldn't recall exactly how many there were an hour, a week later, and if you did it wouldn't really affect your impressions of the room, whether or not you found it to your taste. If you took in 50 per cent of the room it would be a lot, most times considerably less.

Similarly, you don't remember every feature of the face of every person you meet and speak to. And

12

that doesn't matter. Why feel guilty if you miss some details of the novel you're reading?'

DIGBY: 'That makes sense, but if I were reading a business report it. . .'

JAMES: 'But you're not, you're reading a novel. We're talking about the general skills in reading. Using the skiing analogy again, when you first learn to ski you're told to place your weight evenly, bend your knees, lean forward and so on. You aren't shown how to tackle a slalom race.

It's the same with reading. But I'll say this much now, even in a business report there are the key ideas, the meaning words, and the extraneous elaboration you mostly don't need. So the principle remains the same.

Watching Concorde, you don't need to examine all the nuts and bolts to appreciate its aerodynamic shape. If you were to notice only a few of its main features you'd get its message of swift sleekness and power.

As for reading, in the average situation 70 per cent comprehension is all you need. But let me illustrate my point with an example. I'm just going to take any suitable book from my shelf. Here's a biography by Theo Aronson called *Queen Victoria and the Bonapartes*. It's pleasantly readable and informative. It's about the relationship between Queen Victoria and Napoleon III and his wife, Eugenie.

I'll turn to any page. Right, this one – it's taken from the period just after the death of Queen Victoria's consort, Prince Albert. Read it through, as fast as you can, reading for meaning – for the story, the atmosphere, the feel of it and all those other things you listed, colour, movement, etc.'

Digby reads the passage below.

'How one loves to cling to one's grief,' Queen Victoria had once written. Now, clinging to it with all the intensity of her nature, she plunged her Court into its long period of mourning. Had this unrelieved sorrow lasted several months, a year, or even a couple of years, it might have been appreciated and forgiven; but year succeeded year and there seemed to be no light bright enough to pierce the cloud of the Queen's unhappiness. 'The things of this world are of no interest to the Queen . . .' wrote Victoria dolefully to one of her ministers, 'for her thoughts are fixed above.'

If Queen Victoria's thoughts were fixed, as she sighed, 'above', the thoughts of the Emperor Napoleon were fixed, very firmly, below. For as Britain settled down into the long twilight of its Queen's grief, so did France bask in the dazzling sunshine of its Emperor's glory. This decade of Victoria's mourning coincided almost exactly with the most brilliant days of the Second Empire. Rarely, if ever, had the contrast between the Courts of England and France been more pronounced. While Victoria withdrew, almost completely, from her subjects' sight, shunning all public appearances and confining herself to her more remote homes for the greater part of each year, so did Napoleon III spend more and more time in the spotlight. The British monarchy had seldom been more dowdy nor the French more dashing. London, a city without its Sovereign, was like an empty shell; Paris, on the other hand, was *la ville lumière*, the Queen of Cities, the undisputed centre of the civilized world.*

JAMES: 'Now, then, let's look through this piece together. Take a look at the first six sentences. I'll paraphrase them aloud to you.
Sentence 1. Victoria clung to her grief.
Sentence 2. She plunged the Court into its long period of mourning.
Sentence 3. It would have been forgiven if it lasted several months, or a year . . . but it went on and on.
Sentence 4. There . . . no light bright enough to pierce the cloud . . . etc.
The next sentence – her thoughts were fixed above, and the next – Britain settled down into . . . long twilight.
What do all these sentences tell you?'

* From *Queen Victoria and the Bonapartes* by Theo Aronson, Macmillan, New York.

DIGBY: 'About the Queen's long period of mourning.'

JAMES: 'Right. They all say more or less the same thing; how Queen Victoria clung to her grief, that there was no respite, she went on and on. If you had read faster and maybe had not taken in every detail and digested it, you could still have got the feeling of what the first half of the piece was about – the Queen's excessive grief. Follow?'

DIGBY: 'Absolutely.'

JAMES: 'Take the next batch of sentences' (counting) 'seven to be precise.

Sentence 7. In contrast France basked in ... sunshine of the Emperor's glory.

Next, this decade of Victoria's mourning coincided almost exactly ... with brilliant days of the Second Empire.

Next, rarely ... had the contrast between ... been more pronounced.

Next, Napoleon spent more ... time in the spotlight.

Next, London was like an empty shell.

Next, Paris was the Queen of Cities ... and so on. What does all that tell you?'

DIGBY: 'About the contrast between the English and French Courts.'

JAMES: 'Right. And tell me, if you had gone faster and missed some of those details, wouldn't you still receive the whole "message" ?'

DIGBY: 'Yes'.

JAMES: 'And would you remember those details after a while even if you had taken them all in at the time of reading? And would it matter? All you're likely to remember is how the Queen took so long in her mourning and how that made her court contrast with that of Napoleon's.

Rather read two of Aronson's biographies within the same period of time. Incidentally, it has been shown that in any case it's better to read something twice at six hundred words per minute than once at three hundred. More is taken in and recalled from it. So it all points to the need to go faster.'

DIGBY: 'It sounds as if you're suggesting you might as

well read a summary of the book, an abridged version of everything?'

JAMES: 'No, of course not. Selecting your own information is not at all the same as having it summarized for you. You're taking out the information yourself and that's important – you'll be reacting to all that is there. In the same way as you might notice different features of a furnished room, all the things there contribute to your impressions of it.

In reading, each reader will select differently, will take what he feels he wants, will skip differently, if you like, from a mass of evidence. The act of selecting yourself makes it all meaningful. Your 70 per cent comprehension will not be the same as the next person to read the same book. We'll talk about reading digests at a later stage.

But now, let's go through one more passage to consolidate what I'm suggesting, that on no account must you feel guilty about not digesting every detail. That's quite unnecessary, time consuming and to no avail. Right, read through this piece as fast as you can, reading for meaning, and not feeling guilty if you do miss something.'

Digby reads the following passage.

As the years passed, so did the meetings between Victoria and Eugenie fall into a regular pattern. In the summer the Empress would spend a few weeks at Osborne. In the autumn she would stay for a month or so at Balmoral. In the spring the two sovereigns would exchange visits on the Côte d'Azur. At other times during the year, the Empress would spend a few days at Windsor Castle or the Queen would pay her a visit at Farnborough Hill.*

JAMES: 'Now tell me, where would the two women meet in the summer? Where in the autumn, and where in the spring?'

DIGBY: 'I'm not quite sure where at which season. I. . .'

JAMES: 'Good. If you'd answered them all correctly I'd

* From *Queen Victoria and the Bonapartes* by Theo Aronson, Macmillan, New York.

say you were going too slowly. I very much doubt if you'd remember in a month's time, or a week's, the exact answers, and it surely wouldn't matter if you did or didn't. The main message of the piece is that they met quite frequently, in England and in France, and that their friendship must have been important to them.

Exactly the same will apply to any ordinary business article. Let's take a quick example. I'll page through this December 1987 issue of *Business* magazine. In this article, "The DIY End-game", the MD, Jim Hodkinson is discussed. Read this paragraph I'm pointing out, ignoring details.'

Digby reads the following paragraph.

> The driving force behind this growth is Hodkinson. His chauffeur ruefully describes what such success means in personal terms: 'Over the past eight days we've done about 1,200 miles. The day before yesterday, I picked him up at 3 am from a meeting and took him home. I picked him up again at 10 am and we went to the office [B&Q headquarters in Southampton]. At 2 pm I drove him to London for meetings there and brought him back to Southampton at 11 pm. He's killing me.' Hodkinson laughs at the story: 'It was a busy week.' Our interview started at 7 am in the car taking him to work; it ended at 8 pm in the same car when he was on his way home. Colleagues say the frantic pace is nothing unusual.

JAMES: 'Well, I'm sure you can see how the message of Hodkinson's extremely busy day can be taken in without having to register the details of the times and activities of each hour, or distances he travels. That's a complete waste of your time. Would you ever conceivably need to remember any of it?

So, don't feel guilty if you miss some detail unless you have to for a specific purpose, and that's the exception in our daily reading rather than the rule. So try going faster. I realize, of course, there are other faults that are holding you back apart from "word-for-word" reading, but I'll come to those later.

However, I still have something further to say about reading for meaning, and that is, the need to anticipate as you go along. The slightest clue can often tell you what's coming and you can go straight over it. This is an integral part of reading for meaning. The eye only needs to sample cues in a printed piece from the stimulus words. You can predict the rest based on your prior knowledge, a subconscious reconstruction based on previous experience. In general, the first half of a sentence usually gives the foundation for accurate "guessing" in the middle of the sentence.

Words are symbols, marks on paper, their only meaning being that which you give them. If you can catch the meaning for which words are used by the writer not only by not reading every one, but by anticipating some of them, do so. You did when you read that well known phrase about the cat sitting on the mat.

Most of what you read is, after all, written in language similar to that used in conversation, and when conversing with someone you wouldn't, I hope, bore your listener by completing every sentence, or idea, when it is obvious your listener has taken your point. You wouldn't think of describing in detail a coat you want brought to you from among a dozen or more once the cloakroom attendant has already taken yours from the hanger.

In conversation, you'd think I was mad if in discussing the affairs of a well-known personality I was to explain who it was I was talking about... Mother Teresa, who was awarded the Nobel Peace Prize in 1979 for her work among the destitute of Calcutta ... visited Cuba... You know who she is, you don't need to be told. You'd be bored for one thing if I kept doing it. Yet reading that in the newspaper, I take odds on your reading the whole article, the unnecessary part of who she is, which would take up about three lines in an average newspaper column.

Re-using an analogy I made earlier, you wouldn't chew a soft soufflé as diligently as you would a piece of steak just because you were taught to masticate your food well. Don't read words when you already know what they are to be.

Omit any word, phrase, whole sentence even, if you anticipate it, and continue after it. At its simplest level, there are a multitude of familiar phrases that can be anticipated in a flash from the smallest cue, stock phrases in every possible field you can think of. Take the simple political phrases – Act of Parliament; Leader of the Opposition; Prime Minister; political party. You'd be surprised how likely you are to actually let yourself read the entire phrase.

Similarly in business, phrases such as board of directors; managing director; administrative expenses; stock exchange; rates of interest can be recognized by the briefest of cues. Not to mention everyday phrases in their hundreds – in connection with; again and again; up to the present . . . and so on. These, and hundreds like it, crop up in our daily reading – actually to read them is a waste of time and effort.

I've photocopied a short piece, 165 words, from the book *The Skills of Training*, by Leslie Rae, and as you see I've blacked out words and phrases in it. When you read it you must go straight over the gaps, don't stop to fill in words you feel should be there. You won't get the gist of it that way.'

Digby reads the following passage.

1 There is more to training than you think

Some years ago   little problem   defining
training   methods, and   atmosphere
                 conducted. If
               attend   training course
knew   what   expect,   your reactions
     be and   might have   theory
about   learning you would   achieve.
This   pre-knowledge   be enhanced
       course joining instructions,
       detailed programme   exact time

each event   how long each
    title   each   name   speaker.

curriculum vitae   trainers, tutors

                                      domestic information

                                  dress for dinner   lounge
    suits   acceptable   .

JAMES: 'Did you understand it?'
DIGBY: 'Yes.'
JAMES: 'I've blacked out about 30 per cent which you
    didn't need. Of course the actual words any indi-
    vidual brain needs to get the message will vary. I've
    blacked out what *I* don't need. Now look through the
    original article and see if you've missed anything of
    importance by having left out a third of it.'

Digby reads the original.

1 There is more to training than you think

Some years ago there was little problem in defining
training and training methods, and the atmosphere in
which these were conducted. If you were invited,
instructed or nominated to attend a training course you
knew exactly what to expect, what your reactions
would be and you might have had a personal theory
about the learning you would or would not achieve.
This sense of pre-knowledge would be enhanced when
you received your course joining instructions, which
included a detailed programme showing the exact time
of each event during the day and how long each would
last, a title for each event and the name of the speaker.
Also included with the instructions would be a
curriculum vitae of the trainers, tutors or instructors
and the speakers involved in the course. To complete
the comprehensive package, domestic information
would be given including vital information as whether
you would be expected to dress for dinner or that lounge
suits would be acceptable wear during the day.*

* From *The Skills of Training* by Leslie Rae, Gower, Aldershot, 1983.

DIGBY: 'No, I don't think I have missed anything important.'

JAMES: 'Without blacking out the words you need to anticipate what you already know, or what is not necessary to know on that particular occasion.'

DIGBY: 'Isn't that skimming?'

JAMES: 'Not as I consider skimming, which to me involves following a deliberate procedure of approaching reading matter for a specific purpose. But we'll come to that later. I'm talking here of what is considered sensible intelligent reading, getting the meaning from everything you read, but always being aware of and anticipating what is extraneous and unimportant to your general understanding of any particular piece.

What I'm really trying to impress on you yet again is that you mustn't feel guilty about omitting what you've anticipated and what you don't want or need. You are entitled to take what you want from your reading material.

I can't stress it enough. Don't waste time reading what you already know or have anticipated.

As I've already pointed out, you'd be surprised how many unnecessary phrases and whole passages you *do* read, whereas your eyes could anticipate them and flash right over them.

It's the same in real life. You can often recognize a person with whom you are familiar by a single feature such as the eyes, or by a mannerism such as a way of walking. You don't have to scrutinize every feature to know who the person is.

The efficient reader, too, requires fewer clues than the poor reader in order to gain the meaning of a passage. Think of it, you can understand a message with an absolute minimum of words when you've been pushed to it. Take this amusing exchange of telegrams between a father and son:

No mon no fun your son.

Too bad so sad your dad.

So remember to capitalize on anticipating, using as

few clues as you can to understand what you're reading. By the way, what are you reading?'

DIGBY: 'Jeffrey Archer's *Kane and Abel*.'

JAMES: 'Enjoying it?'

DIGBY: 'So-so. I'm not really a best seller reader, but since you suggested I read one. . .'

JAMES: 'I suggested an easy-to-read novel, not necessarily what one calls a best seller. A Steinbeck would have done as well. His writing is clear and simple, yet he's a Nobel prizewinner for literature.'

DIGBY: 'Oh, pity I started the Jeffrey Archer then.'

JAMES: 'Why? Feel guilty now about giving it up?'

DIGBY: 'I guess so – not that I'd have thought of putting it quite that way.'

JAMES: 'Feel you have to finish every book you start?'

DIGBY: 'Generally, yes. I feel I'm giving up, giving in if I don't.'

JAMES: 'Tell me, if you were in the staff canteen and a rather unpalatable plate of goulash was served up, would you eat it all?'

DIGBY: 'Not unless I was starving I suppose, or out of politeness to someone who'd treated me to it.'

JAMES: 'Then why, unless you were stuck on a desert island with nothing but the best seller you're not enjoying, or obliged to read a book written by your best friend, do you feel compelled to continue reading a book you're not interested in or expect to gain anything from?'

DIGBY: 'I've always felt one must persevere.'

JAMES: 'Only till you've given it a reasonable chance surely, and with the average book it doesn't take long to gauge whether the style or contents suit you. So why persist with it if you're not forced to? There are literally thousands of books in the bookshops and libraries that *will* satisfy you. Sheer perseverance for no purpose is pointless. All that happens when you do force yourself, is that you find any excuse to put the book aside, probably halving the amount of reading you would otherwise have got through.

Many worthwhile books, which you feel you should read, are not worth persevering with for too long but give them a chance. They may take a little time to get into, and incidentally, going faster helps you get into them. There are dozens of great books, and if you give up one great one, fiction or non-fiction, in favour of another whose style you prefer, so what? This applies equally in the world of business. Think of all those shelves on selling techniques or management skills that you'll never get around to reading anyway. You might as well go for the ones you do enjoy reading.

Remember, a book must serve *your* purpose, not you the book's. So, if you have your own personal reason for giving up one book and setting off on another, do so – and please stop feeling guilty about it. It's for you to decide what and how to read.

I repeat, the book is there to serve you. You don't owe it the reading.'

DIGBY: 'I'll take your lesson to heart and find myself a different book. Steinbeck sounds a good idea. I haven't read all of his and have enjoyed those I have.'

JAMES: 'Good. We'll leave it at that. See you next week.'

DIGBY: 'Sure, and thanks.'

Summary

Seventy per cent comprehension in one's average reading is adequate.

Do not feel guilty about (*a*) missing details, (*b*) giving up one book in favour of another.

Anticipate wherever possible. Do not read what you know is coming.

Executive action

Continue with your novel (*a*) reading for meaning, (*b*) anticipating words and phrases when you know what they're going to tell you. Anticipate phrases when reading the newspaper.

If you're not enjoying the book you started, put it aside
and get another.

3 Barriers to faster reading

JAMES: 'Well, how's the reading going?'

DIGBY: 'Getting on famously. I'm reading Steinbeck's *The Pearl* and loving it. I'm going faster, I can feel it.'

JAMES: 'And not feeling guilty if you miss a few details?'

DIGBY: 'Certainly not, though there must be times when the details are important.'

JAMES: 'Of course, but that depends on your purpose for reading something. We'll discuss that next week. The first thing to come to grips with is overcoming the barriers to speed. If you've corrected your word-for-word habit, and are now reading for meaning, you've tackled the first hurdle.'

DIGBY: 'And what's the next?'

JAMES: 'Before we start on that, let's take a look at the process of reading. As with any skill, understanding the mechanism behind it helps to improve skills relating to it. In a golf swing, if you understand why you need to transfer your weight, or keep your head still during your swing it makes it easier for you to carry out the actions.

So with reading. Any idea how the eyes work when reading?'

DIGBY: 'Never thought about it to tell the truth, but I suppose they just move smoothly across the lines of print.'

JAMES: 'No, they don't. The eyes can't see while moving.

The result would be a blur, like an overexposed photo of moving cars. They only see as they pause.'

DIGBY: 'How can you tell that?'

JAMES: 'Watch anyone's eyes over the top of a book while they're reading and you'll see the eyes move and pause, move and pause.

You can test it here and now. Hold that pen in your hand at arm's length to one side of you and move it across in front of your vision, keeping your eyes on it but holding your head still.

[Digby carries out the instructions.]

Now *imagine* you're moving it back to its original position. Don't actually move the pen. Keep your head still. What do you feel with regard to your eyes?'

DIGBY: 'They feel as if they're jerking across the imagined path of the pen. I see what you mean, they do work in fits and starts.'

JAMES: 'In reading, the eyes take in a portion of print at each pause or fixation, and then move on to the next portion. The more they take in with each fixation, the less stops and starts they make along a line of print, and therefore the faster they get to the end of a line and passage. Like an express train that gets to its destination sooner than one that has to keep stopping to take in more passengers.'

DIGBY: 'That makes sense, but surely there's not such variation in the amount one is physically able to see at any one time?'

JAMES: 'True, but remember that every contribution to streamlining an activity helps save time and energy. Think of swimmers who shave their legs to save hundredths of a second off their speed, the hair acting as a barrier in the water. Possibly a more realistic analogy is to say that you reach your destination faster if you walk briskly with wide footsteps or even run than if you amble along, stopping every minute.

Getting back to reading – the average reader tends to become lazy, finding it easier to amble, make more fixations than necessary. But you must be efficient in every aspect. Take a simple example, reading car number plates. Practically everyone makes two fixations, seeing the first three letters or numbers and then jumping across to see the next. But it's perfectly easy to see the entire number plate with one fixation. It's a lazy habit, like adding numbers of your fingers, which many people have never trained themselves to overcome. Try when you drive home this evening to take in number plates in one fixation, though don't of course put too much attention to it and bang into the car in front of you. Do the same with road signs. You can generally take in any street sign, names of suburbs etc. with a single fixation.

Then again, reading telephone numbers in the directory; the span is very small. It's not necessary to make two fixations for each.

Now, let's test the idea with words. Here's a list of phrases. Let your eyes read *down* the columns, allowing yourself only one fixation per line. The only sideways movement of your eyes must be from the bottom of one column to the top of the next.'

[Digby carries out instructions on the following list of phrases]

on the team	six out of ten	large storage area
price of gold	please write to	successful small firm
offer a job	supply and demand	plans for the future
try this line	part-time sellers	low profit margins
read it again	please send to	husband-and-wife team

JAMES: 'How did you find it?'

DIGBY: 'The first column was very easy, the second less so and I was sorely tempted to make two fixations in the third column.'

JAMES: 'But could you see each in one fixation when you tried?'

DIGBY: 'Yes.'

JAMES: 'So, do you agree that, with practice, building up the habit of making less fixations will cut out wasteful extra eye movements?'

DIGBY: 'Absolutely.'

JAMES: 'OK. Now read this poem *downwards*, one fixation per line, your eyes moving in one continuous motion. Don't worry about not enjoying it, or missing most of it. I'm trying to get across to you the idea of reading vertically, using single fixations, so that your head moves down the page smoothly.'

Leaving Home

Heartbreaking
Devastating
Immigrating
I weep
I meet strange faces
Places
New home
New road
Dashed hopes
Until I find the ropes
Uprooted tree
And still I leave behind
Some shoots in former soil
Perhaps one small part
Of my soul
In the shattered past
Of my old world.

DIGBY: 'I definitely think I'm faster, but of course it feels stilted, uncomfortable, and obviously I'm not really taking in much of the poem.'

JAMES: 'As you become adept you'll feel happy with it. Give it one more try here before you take the method home. Another little poem, again narrow and wider lines in places. Just read the first three verses.'

Images of an Old Homeland

Remember my land?
Dry sun
Hot land
Yellow veld
Fun for some
Black man on the run
White man holding gun
I remember my land.

Yes, I remember my land
Bright blue skies
Flaming flowers
Swimming pools
Nightly cries
Black man is digging
White man is swinging
Who could forget that land?

Who could forget that land
Enraged black man
With starving young
Ten to a room
Eats from a can
Urban pass for the mass
White man goes first class
Do *you* know my land?

DIGBY: 'I felt very tempted to read across the longer lines.'

JAMES: 'Of course you did. But keep at it, certainly try it out with the narrow newspaper column in the daily press. In most cases, each line is well within the peripheral vision of the reader, but in practice is not read in so streamlined a manner as I'm suggesting.

The important thing is that the eyes are capable of being used in different ways, in this case vertically. We've been trained from the start to zoom in narrowly, over focus if you like, instead of adopting a wider perspective and that is far more tiring for the eyes, as I've already mentioned.'

DIGBY: 'Yes, I remember.'

JAMES: 'To help you get going when reading the newspaper use your index finger, run it down the side of each column, making sure your hand doesn't block the print of the column you're reading. This helps force your eye downwards. But you must keep your finger moving. Try that out for a while till you're into the way of reading downwards.'

[Digby picks up a newspaper and tries it out on an article.]

DIGBY: 'I find it difficult to get the meaning of what I'm reading.'

JAMES: 'I must remind you again, that you'll find you're not taking in the contents as you should for a while. You're learning new skills to replace old ones you've been using every day of your life for decades. You have to suffer for a while.

If you've ever had to relearn a new tennis serve, as I once did, you'll know what I mean. I served dreadfully afterwards till the new serve became my normal one and now I'd find it impossible to revert to the old one.

You use the computer. I'll bet you never found all the instructions, learning the keyboard, the various combinations simple at first. It was probably very muddling. Now your hands fly over it freely, so that you can concentrate on the contents of your work rather than the skills involved in it. It's the same with reading. Keep at it, you'll get into the groove with practice.'

DIGBY: 'I'll try it out on this evening's newspaper.'

JAMES: 'Do that. And now let's look at the next barrier to speed – regression.'

DIGBY: 'Oh yes, that means rereading passages doesn't it?'

JAMES: 'In a sense. But it doesn't mean the legitimate conscious rereading of a passage you genuinely did not comprehend. I'm referring here to the compulsive backflipping, almost a nervous tick, to keep returning to the previous few words because you feel you missed something.

Apart from ruining the forward flow of harmonious reading as it should be, it just isn't necessary. It's not a genuine rereading of a passage you don't understand. You're going back and picking up virtually nothing new from your regression. If you do miss a phrase or two, well, so what? You'd be amazed how much you can miss and still pick up the trail. Ever come late for the cinema? It's rarely a catastrophe, or spoils your enjoyment and understanding of a film if you miss the first few minutes and more.

In conversation, or listening to a speech, you may often miss a few words, or your mind wanders, yet you can bring it back, join in and pick up the thread.'

DIGBY: 'But coming across a difficult word, for instance, one you're not familiar with, sometimes you have to go back and try again at that part of a sentence.'

JAMES: 'For the most part, 90 per cent of the time, treat it as a hurdle in a race, and sprint right over it. It's very seldom that a whole idea will hinge on understanding a single word. Usually the word will be explained in context, the surrounding words allowing you to get the meaning. Reading with a dictionary beside you and stopping at every difficult word is not conducive to active intelligent reading. If you intend to improve your vocabulary, good, but not while you're reading. I'll say more about improving your vocabulary a little later.

For the moment I want to impress upon you the need for forward reading, not regressing. Don't worry about missing something. Could be you haven't missed it in the first place. You've either not registered the few words, somehow sensing they're not important, or you've anticipated them, and then you suddenly feel guilty about it and go back.'

DIGBY: 'More than guilt in this case, I think, is fear that you've missed an important point.'

JAMES: 'Either way you must learn to trust your experience, your "sixth sense", for want of a better expression. You've built up over the decades a vast amount of experience, trust that to tell you intuitively when something is not important.'

DIGBY: 'But surely it is sometimes?'

JAMES: 'Could be. But for the one time you just *may* miss the odd point, you could have picked up far more other important points by getting more read. Statistics show that the average reader regresses ten to eleven times for every one hundred words – 10 per cent of them. That's quite a lot of unnecessary rereading and wastage of time, I'm sure you'll agree.'

DIGBY: 'Certainly sounds it.'

JAMES: 'Remember, as I said before, most of the words in any passage, on their own, have no real meaning.

They're only joining words, keeping the important ones in place, so that a few lost here and there can never materially affect your comprehension of a passage.

Another thing, of course, regression is a form of laziness, encouraging lack of concentration.'

DIGBY: 'Why do you say that?'

JAMES: 'You think of other things and let your mind wander, knowing you can keep going back to get the message you missed. Hence, you don't have to concentrate. But if I tell you to read something and that you're not allowed to regress, but must keep your eyes going ahead of you, you'd just have to concentrate first time around.

So don't worry about what you miss. Don't allow yourself to regress. Have confidence in your ability to get the meaning as you go along. It will save time and increase your comprehension, firstly by forcing you to concentrate and, secondly, by not disturbing the flow of "message" being imparted to you. You disrupt your entire rhythm if you keep regressing, no matter how unconsciously. Train yourself to look ahead in a constant forward motion.'

DIGBY: 'May I try it for a minute or two with my novel? I have it here in my briefcase.'

JAMES: 'Yes, do that. Read it for meaning of course, but concentrate especially this time on not regressing. If your eyes want to go back, tough, don't let them. If you feel you've missed something, too bad, no one will punish you.'

[Digby takes out *The Pearl* and reads it.]

JAMES: 'Well?'

DIGBY: 'I definitely did feel my eyes wanting to go back every now and then. I never allowed them to, but I must admit I took in practically nothing of what I read, concentrating on not regressing.'

JAMES: 'Again, I'm not surprised. You're concentrating on a physical adjustment if you like, which is taking all your attention. I repeat yet again, learning new skills, or worse, unlearning old badly performed skills, will impede your comprehension. Don't worry about it. As your skills improve, you won't have to concentrate on them. You just have too much to think about at this stage. You're relearning a process which you've practised with the same faults for – how many years since you were eight?'

DIGBY: 'I'm sure you're right. I shall keep plugging away.'

JAMES: 'I am right. Let me illustrate from experience in a completely different field. I had to retake my driver's licence in a new country after thirty years of driving. It took me five lessons to get my driving up to scratch for the test. I was a nervous wreck for the first two lessons trying to undo the faults I'd developed over the years. But in the end I developed better driving habits which have stayed with me.

Remember you have to learn each separate act in order to perform them all in unison and smoothly. You can't combine a lot of different skills into one harmonious performance till you're expert at each. Keep practising till it becomes a habit to read correctly. Reading should not be looked on as an intellectual exploit, but as the common everyday necessity it is, like cleaning your teeth. Your comprehension will not only readjust to the new skills, it will improve.

So, when you go on with your novel and any other reading, make a point not to regress. But again, practise on simple material to begin with till it comes naturally and you no longer have to think about it.'

DIGBY: 'OK. So now we move on to the next barrier to speed, I presume?'

JAMES: 'We do, and that's subvocalization. You might have heard of it, a common fault in reading.'

DIGBY: 'I have a vague idea of it.'

JAMES: 'In a nutshell, it's reading aloud, silently.'

DIGBY: 'Let me think about that.'

JAMES: 'It's hearing yourself read in your head. Relying on the sound of words, just as if you were listening to someone reading aloud.'

DIGBY: 'And what's wrong with that?'

JAMES: 'It wastes time and energy.'

DIGBY: 'How?'

JAMES: 'Pronouncing words in your head takes far longer than reacting to the sight of them, which is what you have to aim to do.'

DIGBY: 'Can you explain that with one of your practical analogies?'

JAMES: 'You recognize objects, street signs, all sorts of symbols in your daily life without having to waste time pronouncing them in your head. You just react to the sight of them. Sitting in a train whizzing past fields of sheep, mountains, forests, you don't need to verbalize them to react to them. They arouse feelings in you automatically.'

DIGBY: 'That's easy. They're objects, reality, not a series of symbols like words.'

JAMES: 'What about all the road signs you react to when driving – one-way, no entry, cul-de-sac? They're symbols. In reading at least half the words in print you can recognize automatically, without the need to verbalize them. You can react to how they look, just as you do with familiar signs in everyday life.'

DIGBY: 'I'm not completely convinced.'

JAMES: 'Well I can give you an illustration from reading itself. I'm sure you can recall having read a book where one of the characters has an extraordinarily long or difficult name to pronounce, say Lizaneta Smerdyarshkhaya – that's a classic. Your eyes take in the form, the look of the name, so that when you come across it again, you recognize the character, though the chances are you couldn't repeat the character's name should someone ask you it. In all likelihood you haven't even attempted to pronounce it to yourself. Hasn't that happened?'

DIGBY: 'Oh yes.'

JAMES: 'In that instance you've reacted, recorded the name in your brain as a form, a shape, which is far quicker and more efficient. I'm sure you'll agree that you'd have wasted time if you'd have pronounced it to yourself each time you came across it.'

DIGBY: 'Yes, that makes sense. Now I understand.'

JAMES: 'It's a case of taking this principle further to cover all your reading.'

DIGBY: 'It can't apply to all reading surely? With poetry

and beautiful prose the sound, the rhythms of the words *are* important.'

JAMES: 'Absolutely, in poetry. But that's a very special case. It's like a song – the sound, the tune is important, words are not enough. In "beautiful prose", as you call it, there's room for debate. In "good" literary prose, words are used to create images, put across meaning, they're not used for sound as such. Of course there are exceptions but we're talking in generalities for the most part now, and it's the exception rather than the rule for most writing to need to hear the words. It doesn't apply to most people's daily reading, newspapers, magazines, general fiction.

Too much time is wasted far too often by readers pronouncing and hearing in their heads what they read.

Again, the fault lies largely with our first experiences in reading. The only way the teacher can assess early reading ability is by hearing the child read. At a certain point in the child's development he is told to continue reading to himself, and he goes on in exactly the same way, only noiselessly.

Silent reading is a comparatively recent development. In medieval times very few could read at all. It was for the clergy to master and pass on the teachings to the congregation via oral reading. With the increase in literacy and the printing of books it became convenient for more people to learn to read for themselves and to themselves, the numbers of listeners obviously having a corresponding decline. Silent reading as a common activity before the mid-nineteenth century barely existed. Unfortunately the learning of silent reading is still largely neglected.'

DIGBY: 'Any specific tips on how I should try and eliminate the habit of subvocalizing?'

JAMES: 'Yes, if you're using any part of your body when reading, you must eliminate that.'

DIGBY: 'Using my body?'

JAMES: 'The worst fault, and one you're not guilty of I must add, is using your lips when you read. Watch in the underground some time. You'll be surprised how many people move their lips slightly as they pronounce some of the words.

Watch and see if your kids ever do that. If so, tell them to keep their lips tightly closed, or put a pencil between their lips to keep them from moving. Not between their teeth, mind you, as that still allows the lips to move.'

DIGBY: 'I'll certainly watch them while they read tonight. I can see how that must slow them down.'

JAMES: 'It must do. A second and subtler form of body movement which slows down a reader is using the tongue. Little movements of the tongue that try to read the words orally, while silently. Regrettably I'm guilty of that at times, when I'm very tired. When I become aware of it, I shake myself up, tell myself to get along. I consciously stop using my tongue and I can feel myself going faster.

Only on rare occasions when I'm reading something very difficult, I find it does help to use my tongue. As I've said, the senses are related. One does, in exceptional circumstances, need all the help one can get from all one's senses. But, that is very rarely necessary.'

DIGBY: 'How can I stop myself from doing it?'

JAMES: 'Keep your tongue firmly against the roof of your mouth as if it's stuck there. You'll soon feel if you want to use it. A useful test to see if you are using it is to chew gum, or anything else for that matter, and see if it interferes with your comprehension, in which case you'll know you're in the habit of using it to help you read. When at any time you become aware of the habit, force yourself to stop and you'll immediately feel yourself reading faster, unhampered by any physical movements.

If you like, try it. Read a few paragraphs, or pages in your novel, deliberately using your tongue and then read a further page or so keeping it still.'

[Digby does so.]

DIGBY: 'I get the point. I can easily feel the difference.'

JAMES: 'There's an even subtler form of body movement

that can occur in reading. If you place your fingers lightly on the sides of your neck you might become aware of slight muscle movement beneath your fingers either side of your larynx. A sign you're using your body to read. And that is taboo when you read silently. I must warn you that you'll find this the most difficult barrier to overcome. You can't completely eradicate hearing yourself, but you must cut down on it.

Read again from your novel for a couple of minutes concentrating on not subvocalizing. Go faster just to ensure you're not using your tongue or hearing too many words. Don't worry overmuch about not comprehending as well as you should.'

[Digby reads for two minutes.]

DIGBY: 'It's more difficult than I thought it would be. I can't stop myself "hearing" words.'

JAMES: 'Just keep at it. Practice makes perfect, as they say.'

DIGBY: 'I seem to have so much to think of I feel quite lost.'

JAMES: 'Have faith Digby, trust me. It *is* muddling with so much to think of. Your comprehension must be affected, not to mention your pleasure in reading, but I assure you, yet again, it will all come together and then you won't know yourself. Just concentrate on the three barriers we've discussed:

    reading for meaning
    not regressing
    reducing subvocalization.

You'll cut your reading time by half or more in many instances, and think what that means. Every ten hours of work-related material you read at the moment, will be reduced to five or less, giving you hours more to do other things, for leisure reading, or that extra game of golf. It's worth working for so please don't be disheartened.

Well, that's more than enough for today. We'll leave it there. But keep practising. No typist masters the keyboard without practising to build up speed.

One of the great musicians, I forget who, once said that if he missed one day's practice he noticed it, if he missed two his teacher did, and if he missed three, his audience did. So keep on plugging away. Without realizing it you'll be improving and, though you might not believe me now, once you've become streamlined in your reading skills, you'll never be able to go back to your old bad habits. I'll give you a chance to test that out later.'

DIGBY: 'That should be interesting.'

JAMES: 'There is one more thing. I said I'd bring up the subject of vocabulary again. Although there's no need to over-worry about words while reading, I don't want you to feel that a good, powerful vocabulary isn't something to strive for. The more varied it is, the more it facilitates your reading at all levels. The extent of your vocabulary, whether you approve or not, is used as an indicator of your intelligence and ability. Most intelligence and aptitude tests require a reasonably proficient vocabulary and the way you express yourself in interviews, presentations and so on, will surely be noted. Therefore, I'd like you to make a conscious effort to increase your vocabulary, because tests have shown that without this specific effort little growth is evident in an adult's span of words after his student days. And here I'm referring to the extent of a person's vocabulary as his ability to use a word.'

DIGBY: 'You mean speak it?'

JAMES: 'Or be able to use it in writing. We can all cope with more words passively, that is listening to or reading them, though we'd be hard pressed at times to say what they mean.'

DIGBY: 'I'm often caught out by my children that way.'

JAMES: 'I know the feeling. I'm sure you must come across words every now and then that you'd like to use yourself but just can't be sure you'll be using them correctly, in fact, you don't know their real meaning?'

DIGBY: 'Oh of course. One that comes to mind is "esoteric". I often read the word and am never really sure what it means so I'd never use it.

JAMES: 'We'll use that as an example. What you should do is keep a pack of small index cards in a tickler box for convenience. On each card in bold letters, write the word in the centre. So. . . [taking up a pen and writing]

| ESOTERIC |

On the back of the card write a dictionary definition and a sentence using the word. Give the word its most common use – esoteric means "made for, or understood by only a small select group". You could use the sentence "Astrology used to be an esoteric subject, now most people dabble in it".

Place the completed card in alphabetical order in your tickler box, along with those other words which pop up periodically which you'd like to feel confident to use.

When you have an odd minute, once a week even, go through the cards and see if you can recall the definition and sentence of each word. When you've used the word in your own speech, discard the card – you'll have mastered the word. You'll feel rather good when you use one you've never been able to use before.'

DIGBY: 'Sounds a good idea. I can think of a couple of words right now that I might find useful.'

JAMES: 'Well, try it out. Now we must call it a day. Next week we'll go into the other side of reading, the mental approach.'

DIGBY: 'But all reading is mental, according to you.'

JAMES: 'True. I'm glad you've learned that lesson. But, what I mean is reading as an activity – the correct approach to reading, apart from the actual skills of the physical process.'

DIGBY: 'I look forward to that.'

JAMES: 'Good. See you.'

Summary

Read vertically whenever possible in single fixations,

Do not regress. Keep a constant forward movement of your eyes.

Cut down on subvocalization. Rely on the sight of the words rather than their sound. Go faster to eliminate subvocalization.

Make a conscious effort to increase your vocabulary by using index cards.

Executive action

Practise reading vertically – narrow newspaper columns.
Use single fixations for reading – street signs and directions
– motor car number plates
– telephone numbers in directory.
Read your novel – with meaning + no regressing + limited subvocalization. Keep your tongue firmly against roof of mouth or on floor of mouth.
Keep a file of index cards to gather words with which you are not familiar. Once you have used them freely in speech, discard the relevant card.

4 Fixing your purpose

DIGBY: 'I find I'm enjoying my reading more now and I'm not falling asleep over my book at night. I have to consciously put it aside and turn out the lights.'

JAMES: 'Good. And are you still reading *The Pearl*?'

DIGBY: 'No, no. I got through that in no time, it's simply written. I'm reading one of Theo Aronson's biographies, *Grandmama of Europe*, having also read and enjoyed his *Victoria and the Bonapartes* so much. I'd never have got through so much in the old days when I was ploughing through every page, worrying about every detail in every sentence. You're absolutely right. I've learnt quite a lot about Victoria and the Bonaparte relationship, though I can't record exact details of each occasion on which they met. I see that it's not important in the general scheme of things. After all, I told myself, I can't remember what each person said and looked like at every function I attend.'

JAMES: 'So you're over the guilt bit about detail?'

DIGBY: 'Mostly.'

JAMES: 'I'm very pleased to hear it. It's one of the biggest hurdles to cross.'

DIGBY: 'But I presume there's a lot more to learn. I doubt if I'll be able to spin along so fast and carefree with my work-related material.'

JAMES: 'No, you can't read everything at the same speed or in the same way. That's what we're coming to now, reading effectively. Time-managing your

41

reading doesn't mean racing along over everything at the same high speed. There's no one speed at which you can, or should, read everything. You must be flexible. That's why, as I've said before, I dislike the term "speed reading". A conscious flexibility in speed is the hallmark of the proficient reader. A poor reader plods along reading everything at more or less the same speed.'

DIGBY: 'Surely everyone varies speed – goes faster, for instance, when reading an exciting story than when reading a difficult theoretical treatise on business management, or a subject one's not interested in?'

JAMES: 'That's not quite what I mean. I deliberately chose the word *conscious* flexibility. Your variation in speed from, say, a narrative to a philosophical tome would be an automatic reaction to the material you're reading. The material is dictating to you how you read it.

This is not good enough. It's like a poor tennis player with no control over the ball who merely returns it as he is forced to, rather than selects a deliberate stroke and placement for his return.

To read efficiently you must consciously select your own speed and vary it to suit your purpose in choosing the material in the first place. Why are you reading it? That should come first, rather than what the material is.'

DIGBY: 'I need to think about that.'

JAMES: 'Take a simple analogy. Normally, as a driver, you take care when motoring along busy winding roads. But suppose you're taking someone to hospital who's bleeding to death? You'd race along – your purpose would determine your speed, though the state of the road (or printed matter in reading) would affect you. Similarly, no matter how empty the road, how straight and direct it is, you'd drive very slowly if you were peering through the high grass in a game reserve hoping to spot some hidden animals.'

DIGBY: 'So I must deliberately choose how to read something?'

JAMES: 'Yes. Much like a golfer selects the correct club for each shot – a wood for a long shot, a short iron when he's close to the green. He'll never just walk and hit without thinking primarily of what he's trying to achieve, and what he expects to encounter during the course of it. The better the player, the more deliberate the choice of method in play. The same with a reader.'

DIGBY: 'But surely you can't deny that the text must affect the way you get through it?'

JAMES: 'Of course, same as the layout of a particular hole for the golfer, or conditions such as wind will affect him, so the material being read will affect the reader, if it's easy or difficult. But in the first instance it's the purpose, what you want from the material, that's important.

I must stress that it's your purpose which must determine your choice of speed and manner of reading. This is the beginning of *active* reading.'

DIGBY: 'Active reading?'

JAMES: 'Yes. Reading, you'll agree, is an activity and therefore all readers must be actively involved in the process. You're about to interrupt and say that's obvious, but, without realizing it, most of us are guilty to some extent of considering reading a passive pastime. The writer is considered to have done all the work while we readers sit back and receive the information.'

DIGBY: 'Now that you say that. . .'

JAMES: 'In communication of any kind, both the giver of information and the receiver must be actively involved in the whole activity.

In a telephone conversation, you must listen actively in order to respond correctly. You may find yourself saying "That's nice" when boring old Mr Blobbs tells you he's broken his finger, because you're not listening actively to him.

Let's take a sporting analogy again. Think of a game where one player starts the movement of the ball and another ends it – cricket or baseball, for example. Both players are equally active. If the catcher were only to hold up his hands in the air waiting for the ball to fall into them, it would need a computer to calculate the odds of his catching it.

He has to use his head, judge from the way the ball is bowled or pitched, how it's batted and so on, and prepare himself to catch the ball in the best possible way.

In the same way, a reader has to put active skill into his reading if he's to "catch" the meaning of what a writer has presented to him.'

DIGBY: 'That's very interesting. You're right, one does tend to think of the writer being more active than the reader when both meet on the common ground of the material between them. But how does one became an active reader?'

JAMES: 'By asking questions – of yourself and of all the material you are to read. Ask the right questions in the right order. This is the essence of active reading.'

DIGBY: 'What are these questions?'

JAMES: 'There are five of them, the depth varying in accordance with the level of material you're reading. Remember, ask no questions, get no answers. The answers will be in direct relationship to the amount of thinking and analysing you do yourself.

I've written down the five questions for you. Look through them and then we'll discuss each one in turn.'

[James hands the following typed sheet to Digby.]

Five questions in active reading

1 Why am I reading this book/chapter/article, and what do I hope and expect to gain from it?

2 What is the main theme/message/point of what I'm reading? What does the author wish me to learn from it?

3 How is the theme, the skeleton fleshed out, constructed and developed in detail?

4 What is my reaction, i.e. my criticism of it?

5 Was it worth reading, i.e. what is its significance in the light of what I wanted and expected from it?

JAMES: 'We'll look at each question in turn. The first is

to be asked of yourself: Why am I reading this piece and what do I hope and expect to gain from it?

Only by knowing what you want from a selection and what you anticipate learning from it can you decide how to read it, if in fact to read it at all. An efficient reader has a clearly defined purpose of why he's reading a particular piece and what he expects to gain from it.

After all, you do this in other aspects of your daily life. If you want a relaxing sunshine holiday you select a seaside resort. If you want an active winter holiday you choose a ski resort in the mountains. You know why you've chosen that particular place and what you expect from it. This will determine how you approach it, what clothes to take and so on.

This approach is equally essential in all forms of communication. If you choose to watch a light comedy when you're tired, and land up seeing a slow, obscure film you might well fall asleep, though on another occasion you'd enjoy it. Then you'll have wasted your time and energy, and probably money into the bargain.

So it is with reading. You must define your purpose before settling to read anything. What do you want from it – light entertainment, escape, some bare facts about a current event, to master the details, to find answers to specific problems? Once this is established you can select the correct "gear" of speed in which to read, each gear for a particular type of read.

Remember, reading is a mental activity. You must read as fast as your mind demands.'

DIGBY: 'And you must stick to your purpose, no doubt, all the way through your reading?'

JAMES: 'Yes, keep it firmly and concisely in your mind throughout.

As I said, all this leads to different "gears" of reading. Sir Francis Bacon summed it up well when he said: "Some books are to be tasted, others to be swallowed, and some few to be chewed and digested". More important than the right technique or method is knowing the approach for achieving a particular result.'

DIGBY: 'That all makes sense, and I accept you need a purpose when reading, but how do you know whether or not a piece answers your purpose till you've read it?'

JAMES: 'A fair question. You find out if it serves your purpose by previewing it, before reading it. That'll save you from ploughing through miles of print in books, journals, magazines and newspapers, only to recognize too late that you've wasted your time and energy and gained nothing of what you had hoped or wanted. Reading involves selecting and discriminating, not wholesale absorption, and the first step is to select carefully what you're going to spend time reading and to discard that which won't answer your purpose. It'll also tell you how you'll read what you do select.'

DIGBY: 'Do you preview everything?'

JAMES: 'Yes, to a larger or lesser extent. Some previewing, pre-reading, is essential as an aid to defining your purpose. You need to know what book or article you're reading as early as possible. This applies to all written material – technical, exposition, fiction. You need a bird's eye view, a survey which will determine whether you go ahead and read it or not, and the way you read it. Also it'll help you focus your attention and concentration on it if you do decide it's worth reading.

Take again our example of selecting a vacation. You wouldn't go on a holiday without finding out something about the place, its climate, its activities, if you have to wear a tie for dinner, in order to assure it suits your purpose. Then you can prepare yourself and get the most from the holiday.

Similarly, when driving on a long journey if you're sensible you'll study a map before you leave so that you'll know at which exit to leave the motorway. You'd plan for it in order to avoid wasting time, energy and petrol driving miles past your destination, or causing some disruption by having to pull up alongside a busy highway and rummage through your maps. Planning ahead in everything always helps.'

DIGBY: 'I never go to see a film without knowing something about it beforehand, either by watching the trailer or reading or hearing a review by someone whose opinion I value. I suppose that's a type of preview.'

JAMES: 'Yes, and it's the same with reading. You need to size up the reading material in your hand, to "shop around". When you're choosing a new car, certain features determine whether or not you buy it. Look at the main characteristics of a book, chapter, article, and that will determine whether or not you continue with it or put it aside.'

DIGBY: 'You're not going to tell me to judge a book by its cover are you?'

JAMES: 'Don't underestimate the significance of a book-cover in your selection process. There's a psychology behind all packaging. The cover of a book is designed to appeal to a type of readership. Compare, for example, the sensitive covers of those thought-provoking feminist novels, each individually created, to those for mass-produced, lightweight romances.

Taking work-related examples, different covers suggest different types of book. For example, a cover with just a title suggests a more academic approach than one with an illustration. Also in general, a cover showing a graph suggests a practical application to the subject-matter.

But getting back to previewing a book, in some cases a preview will provide all the information you need, in which case you can put it aside and for all practical purposes you've completed your reading of the work at thousands of words per minute – for what it's worth to you. Now you're over the guilt bit about giving up a book, putting it aside would be no problem. As someone said to me, some books are to be put aside, some to be hurled away with force. The sooner you discover which, the better.

However, the pre-reading might strengthen your motive to continue and even then previewing won't have been a waste of time because, as has been shown in various tests, it paves your way for a speedier and more comprehensive coverage, fixing an overall schema in your mind.

Never forget, a book is there to serve your purpose – not the other way around.'

DIGBY: 'And no doubt you suggest a specific way of previewing?'

JAMES: 'I do. Too many people grab at a book, look at the title and the blurb and plunge right in. This is haphazard, inefficient and a waste of time and energy. There is a methodical way to preview everything you read, from an entire book to a short article.

Incidentally, did you preview the biography you're reading at the moment?'

DIGBY: 'I didn't feel I needed to with this one.'

JAMES: 'Why not?'

DIGBY: 'I enjoyed *Victoria and the Bonapartes*, so starting another by the same author was good enough for me.'

JAMES: 'Maybe in this instance it's excusable, but remember that authors can change style or outlook at different periods of their life, so that's not really good enough as a rule. But let's go through the steps you should take in previewing all written material, fiction and non-fiction. Firstly, read the title. That's stating the obvious, but think about the title, especially in non-fiction. Although the title of a novel is less indicative of what's inside, it can often tell you a lot. Some titles sound more "creative", more thought-provoking than others. The titles of Muriel Spark's novels have been considered minor triumphs themselves, often chosen before the book is written. I personally am influenced by the name of a book, just as I form some sort of picture of the type of people I meet by the names they give their children – made-up ones, fashionable ones, solid enduring ones.

A non-fiction title can be very important. Spare a moment to consider it and make a quick judgement at what it aims to tell you. It is a clue to the topic of discussion and can often give essential information about a book or article before you start to read it.

Consider the implications of two books entitled "A Method of Training Today" and "The Method of Training Today". Much as "The Story of Mankind" is very different from "A Story of Mankind". That's the sort of thing to look out for.

After reading the title, read the blurb. There's nothing more irritating to me than taking a book from the library shelf and finding that the blurb is missing.'

DIGBY: 'But the blurb is no true reflection of a book. It's written to promote it and must put it in the best light.'

JAMES: 'If a book says nothing of importance, be sure the blurb reflects this. A blurb which is only a puff, using glittering generalities about how "stupendous, marvellous, thrilling . . ." the book is, and nothing more, suggests clearly that there is nothing much to it.

Now read the name of the publisher, and the country of publication. In non-fiction, is it by a well-known or obscure publisher? Is it a publisher you respect in the particular field you're reading? Is it also important for your purpose or the subject-matter whether the book has first been published in the UK or in the US for instance?

In fiction also, the name of the publisher can be significant, possibly suggesting a certain image. And the country of first publication is significant. Styles of writing vary enormously from one country to another, and therefore may play a role in your selection of a book.

It's personal preference in what order you carry out the steps in previewing. This will tend to vary with what you're looking for. For me the next step, generally, is to look at the date of publication. This is very important in a non-fiction, yet often omitted by a reader. *Is* it a new book, or an updated edition? If it's unrevised it could be of limited use when not recent. Note the number of reprints; if there are many, the book must have been well received.

The date of publication can also be of importance in fictional works. Do you want to read a book written in the eighteenth century, the nineteenth century, or in the present? It also sets you in the period in which the writer lived and worked. It helps to give you a perspective. For example, in a work of science fiction, you'll expect quite a different slant in a book written sixty years ago compared with one written today.'

DIGBY: 'What about the author? You haven't come to the importance of the writer yet.'

JAMES: 'I'm about to. Of course it's most important to consider the writer no matter how briefly. Again, what aspect of the writer is of value to you varies according to whether the book is a work of fiction which you're reading for pleasure, or non-fiction where your aim is to be instructed, even if it is for your pleasure. In the case of non-fiction you're reading exposition, which is informing you about something and you need to know if the writer has the experience necessary to have written success-fully in the field in question. What are his or her qualifications, past record? If you're forced to choose one book on a specific subject, its safer to select an author who appears to fill the bill.'

DIGBY: 'And a fiction writer – how does knowing about him or her help you choose a book, apart from one who's been recommended or one you know?"

JAMES: 'The life experience, background or education of a particular author may arouse interest in you as prospective reader, or kill it. True, you could miss a good book by not taking to the "sound" of the writer, but when you're faced with dozens of similar looking books on a shelf, you've a better chance of success at a deliberate selection surely?'

DIGBY: 'That makes sense. If a writer has had an inter-esting life, judging from the blurb, the chances are this will come through in the book.'

JAMES: 'As you say, you'll have more of a chance going for that writer than one who makes no impact on you. I've found, what's more, that knowing some-thing about the writer's life adds to my understanding and appreciation of his or her work. Of course, not too much of that comes out in a blurb, but it's worth bearing in mind. Certainly with the great writers, understanding their life helps and it's often valuable picking up the odd book that gives you some real background to a writer. But we won't go into that. We'll now take a look inside the book.'

DIGBY: 'I suppose you're going to mention the preface, introduction and foreword.'

JAMES: 'Yes, and I'm sure you're about to say you don't always bother about them.'

DIGBY: 'You're right. I often give them a miss.'

JAMES: 'Not a good idea. Read them. They give the notion of the book, tell you what it's about and provide valuable clues for the reader. Remember they're usually the last things written, although they appear in the front of a book. The writer takes the trouble to inform you, give you a preview of some sort for a purpose, so the reader who ignores them is likely to waste time reading what he could have discovered almost immediately was not for him.

Take a simple example. In the preface a writer may talk of "birdwatching" or "ornithology". Which is more likely to be for the amateur? Likewise, which would be more for the amateur collector of mineral specimens – a book written for "rockhounds" or "mineralogists"? These are the sort of clues the intelligent previewing reader can pick up.'

DIGBY: 'But some of them are so long.'

JAMES: 'Well, preview them at least, but don't ignore any introduction, foreword, or preface altogether. And include in your preview any contents list or index to select in the first place.'

DIGBY: 'I must say the list of steps in previewing seems rather long.'

JAMES: 'Not when you put them into practice. They save time in the end. One last step to take if the book passes all the other tests, and that is pick up a taste of the style by dipping in here and there throughout the book, sample the vocabulary and judge if it suits you. Notice the length of paragraphs. Each one is a unit of thought in which a single idea is developed.

If they're short paragraphs, it's a reliable indication that the book has many ideas and is not heavy in detail. Long paragraphs suggest more detail therefore making the book more difficult to read.

Remember, there are dozens of books on every conceivable subject, so where time is valuable you must use every aid you can to select the correct book for your need.'

DIGBY: 'James, I see the value in everything you've said, particularly for a single book on one subject, but what about articles in journals and magazines?'

JAMES: 'Ah yes! I've some very valuable advice on how to preview articles, but we haven't time this session. We'll do that next week. In the meantime put into practice the steps we've discussed in selecting all the books you're considering reading.'

DIGBY: 'I'll go through the list of books for XX, though I suppose you previewed them before giving the list to me?'

JAMES: 'Not really, I left that to you. I did some very superficial selecting. You might find that some of the material is of more value to you than others. Start with those. And preview everything from now on.'

DIGBY: 'I'll remember that. In fact before I go I think I should write down the list of steps in previewing just to keep handy.'

JAMES: 'I'll itemize them for you. You can vary the order as you wish. Eventually it'll become automatic for you to preview correctly, you won't have to think about it.

So, for previewing books you need to take note of: the title; author; blurb; name of publisher; date of publication; any preface, introduction, or foreword; Style and vocabulary; contents list, and index.'

DIGBY: 'Right, I've written that down.'

JAMES: 'You'll find next week, when we discuss a way to preview articles, how really valuable previewing can be. But I'll say no more now. See you next Wednesday.'

DIGBY: 'Thanks, see you then.'

Summary

Read actively by asking five questions of everything you read:

1   Why am I reading this book/chapter/article, and what do I hope and expect to learn from it?
2   What is the main theme/message/point of what I'm reading? What does the author want me to learn from it?
3   How is the theme constructed and developed in detail?
4   What is my reaction to the piece? What is my criticism of it?
5   Was it worth reading? That is, what is its significance in the light of what I wanted and expected from it?

Question 1 establishes your purpose in reading something, which will in turn suggest to you what 'gear' or speed you should read it at.

As an aid to establishing your purpose preview everything.

With every book look at and note: title, author, blurb, publisher, date of publication, any preface, introduction, foreword, contents list, and index.

Test for style and vocabulary.

Executive action

Preview several non-fiction books on a particular topic and decide in order of preference which ones you think will give you the 'best return' for that subject-matter. If possible read them afterwards to test how helpful your previewing has been.

Look through a few novels in a bookshop or library and preview them. Decide, in order of preference, which of them you are more likely to enjoy.

5 Previewing articles

DIGBY: 'I must say, James, I have found that previewing
helps. With the XX project I did just what you said,
looked through all the features you'd listed and I
feel I've come up with the best from the selection of
books on the subject.'

JAMES: 'I'm pleased to hear it, but not surprised, mind
you. I know it helps to preview.'

DIGBY: 'I'm still having difficulty in selecting articles
from the journals, and I wasted time in reading some
quickly, though I know we're getting onto that
today.'

JAMES: 'We are, and I'm going to show you a marvellous
way to preview articles efficiently, a step-by-step
guide. I call it the "3T Method of Preview" – top,
trail and tail. We'll deal with each in turn.

Step 1, *top* it. Note all the general features of the
article. Read its title, check as far as possible that
it covers the desired subject. Bear in mind the nature
of the magazine in which it appears. For example,
a business article in a women's home magazine is
likely to be simpler than one from a sophisticated
scientific journal. *Business* magazine articles are
likely to be simpler than those from the *Harvard
Business Review*, and so on. You know that magazines reflect the nature of the market but you'll be
surprised how often readers don't take that into
account in their approach to any particular article.
It should prepare you by telling you if its likely to

be at the level you want, what that level is, and therefore what "gear" of speed you should use.

Note the length of the article and the date of publication. Is it recent? Read any blurb or summary alongside the article, usually in bold print.

Note the author. Are there any comments referring to him or her?

That completes the "topping": title of article, nature of the magazine, its length and the date of publication, and summary/foreword.

Step 2, *trail* it. As the word suggests, you trail through, starting by reading the first paragraph. That generally states the thesis or main point of the article. Occasionally, if you feel the main point has not been made, read the second paragraph. On the other hand, if you understand the thesis from the first part of the opening paragraph, don't complete it.

Next, read the subheadings, and the first sentence of each following paragraph. Again, if the first sentence is very long and you've got the message of it half way through, don't bother to finish it.'

DIGBY: 'Why the first paragraph?'

JAMES: 'Because, at least 80 per cent of the time, it's the first sentence that states the gist, the topic point of the paragraph. We'll look into that again later, for the moment accept the method.

Step 3, *tail* it. Read the last paragraph as you did the first. Generally it contains the summary or conclusion, the review of the writer's central idea.'

DIGBY: 'I'll just make a quick note of those steps.'

JAMES: 'I'll give you a short summary of what to do.'

[He hands Digby a typed sheet.]

'The best way to test the method, of course, is to put it into practice. Let's do that now.

I want you to imagine you're in the dentist's waiting room, with only a few minutes before being called in to see him. There's one magazine available, *Working Woman*. You page through and see an article entitled "What to do when you're feeling blue". You are feeling blue, so you think maybe you can pick up some quick advice on how to get out of your depression. The chances are you don't have time to read the whole article, nor is there any point, necessarily, if it isn't going to help you. You'd rather read something else. What do you do?'

DIGBY: ' "3T Preview" it.'

JAMES: 'Right, you don't waste time and energy reading it. It's about 2,500 words long, which would take the average person more than ten minutes to read. Even at twice the average reading rate, say 400 words per minute, you'd still need five minutes which you may not have. Here's the article.'

[James passes the article across to Digby, who previews it – see pages 57–60.]

JAMES: 'Now let's discuss your previewing of it step by step. First, "topping" it. The title, any comments?"

DIGBY: 'Pretty clear, it intends telling you what to do when you're feeling low.'

JAMES: 'And that's what interests you sitting there in the waiting room, feeling blue yourself?'

DIGBY: 'Yes.'

JAMES: 'So your purpose, keeping that to the fore of your mind, is to get some advice on what to do when feeling low, and that's what you expect from it.'

[Digby nods.]

'The title of the magazine, *Working Woman*, how does that strike you?'

DIGBY: 'The topic is general, so I'd presume the same principles would apply to men and women.'

JAMES: 'Anything else about the magazine to consider, no matter how briefly?'

DIGBY: 'It's not likely to be obscure, difficult to read in the limited time I'd have.'

JAMES: 'Notice the length of the article?'

DIGBY: 'Yes, not too long to cope with.'

JAMES: 'You'll also learn, incidentally, to judge the number of words in an article.'

DIGBY: 'You did send me particulars on how to measure that.'

[See Appendix.]

What to do when you're feeling BLUE

Everyone gets depressed – and everyone wonders *why*. But in her new book Dr Audrey Livingston Booth, director of the Stress Foundation, looks not at the causes of depression but at the cures: simple everyday steps we can all take to avoid that sinking feeling

'Take a deep breath and walk, walk, walk. . . .'

It's the sort of buck-up advice you might expect to hear a nanny of the old school urging on to her mopey charges. It wouldn't be fair to say that it summarised the essential stress philosophy of Dr Audrey Livingston Booth, director of the Stress Foundation, but it does give a jolly good whiff of it.

Brisk and breezy, she is an energetic, beaming woman who carries her learning lightly – lots of letters after her name denoting numerous academic qualifications in psychology, sociology and health education – but one who obviously believes strongly in practising what she preaches. Swimming, walking, relaxing, eating wholesome food, enjoying the company of family and friends, doing the things she's always done – 'You should never stop doing what you enjoyed when you were young' – are all packed into a very busy working life. Stress is part of the schedule and she admits she is always hovering near her peak point, but she's lucky enough to have the kind of personality that thrives rather than wilts on being stretched.

No stranger to stress of a more serious kind – she survived two very fraught marriages before her present happy one – she writes as she speaks, incisively but warmly, too, and with sympathy. 'Pamper yourself,' she insists. 'You can never be too concerned with yourself.' In her book, *Stressmanship* (Severn House Publishers, £4.95), from which the extract on pages 58 to 60 is taken, she makes it clear that 'Know yourself' is also essential for those who would learn to harness stress rather than be driven by it.

When she established her Stress Foundation a few years ago, and got together a very eminent group of people to sit on the Board of Trustees and the Scientific Advisory Council, she quickly found out that there was already more than enough research into both the causes and the results of stress. A pragmatist to the core, she promptly set about filling the obvious gap, which was to interpret all that material and create some practical programmes to put her theories to the test.

Today she runs in-company courses for managers, teaching people to recognise stress in themselves and others and how to handle it. She is very keen to train the trainers in these techniques, beause she feels that rather than use the outside expert, middle managers should

This article is reproduced from *Working Woman*, November 1985. (This magazine is no longer in print.)

be trained in stress recognition as part of their job. Coping with stress is currently flavour of the month in management training, but I doubt if there's anyone to match her expertise and experience in the field.

She's utterly convinced that if we followed her advice we could all live out a healthy, happy century. Maybe that's not everyone's ideal but neither is it the wishful thinking of a crank. Everything that Dr Audrey advocates for the management and reduction of stress is based on a sound understanding of the body/mind interaction. It's this knowledge, liberally laced with her engaging optimism, which makes her book such rollicking fun to read. It's also peculiarly instructive.

She will have none of the doom and gloom 'do-this-or-you'll-die' approach to stress so often adopted by the medical experts. Typically, to make sure the reader is getting the point, every paragraph is headlined in the margin. Now this is sometimes rather irritating, but the method has its advantages. Since most of what she writes is practical, with even the theoretical sections being closely linked to application through the use of charts and questionnaires, and since, depending on the kind of personality you discover yourself to be, you have to track your way through different chapters for the appropriate guidance, this underlining of points serves as a useful aid for reference.

Depression is one reaction to stress and afflicts many more people than actually seek alleviation for it. It's also more prevalent among women than men, as we know from the NHS tranquilliser bill. Audrey surmises that this is partly because women on the whole are physically much more overloaded than men, which can make them feel inadequate or unable to cope with the demands put upon them; partly, she thinks, it's a female tendency to internalise feelings of hurt, rejection or anger.

But, she says firmly, providing it is not severely clinical, there are ways of handling it yourself. 'You've got to find your spirit lifter,' she says. 'Mine is Hungarian music played very loud' – pause – 'd'you know, I've just realised I haven't got a single record in my repertoire. Now that's sheer bad management.'

When the stress is high and the adrenaline low, she advises a 'do nothing' policy. 'I always tell people to steer clear of newspapers and the box. It's not escapist. We've got enough problems to contend with in our private lives without taking on the cares of the world. Don't even buy a cat.' ●

■HOW MANY KINDS OF DEPRESSION ARE THERE?
There are several. Some are part of our normal swings. We have 'ups' when we feel we could climb Everest, win a beauty contest or conquer the world, and we have 'downs' when nothing at all seems to go right for us. These I call having a down day and having a fit of the blues.

The down day is a very short spell of feeling down in the doldrums. It can be triggered off by something quite simple like oversleeping yet again, and is just as quickly dispelled by something nice happening to us. A cheerful 'good morning' from a neighbour can make the spirits soar again.

A fit of the blues lasts longer, perhaps two or three days, and may occur simply because the body is fighting some infection and is not doing too well in the battle. We, of course, are not conscious of this; we only know that we feel low and 'under par'. It may also occur through a rebuff, through a row with a close friend, or work may get on top of us and we feel, temporarily, that life is all work and no play. Sooner or later, though, our spirits lift and we forget that we have ever felt blue.

For women, depression may occur as the body chemistry changes before a period, after the birth of a baby and again at the change of life when childbearing comes to an end. The feeling of failure is also a prime trigger for depression. The failure of not being able to achieve a satisfying sexual life or a longed-for child or a successful career for which one previously trained are prime examples. Similarly, failure to achieve success as a wife and mother can cause depression, particularly if one's children turn to glue sniffing, drugs or socially unacceptable behaviour.

■THE REAL DEPRESSIONS
There are the real depressions, though, which are definitely illnesses and they both need recognising and treating. They are of two main types: reactive depression and endogenous depression.

RE-ACTIVE DEPRESSION is triggered off by things which cause us distress. It might be the loss of our job, of our love, or of our standing in the community. It could be failure to succeed at things which are important to us. It is also sometimes triggered off by our failure to do our best. People in all walks of life suffer from this pressure of time and overload of work, while at the other end of the scale those who have lost their jobs suffer from depression through sheer frustration and hopelessness. Reactive depression, as its name implies, is depression caused by our reaction to these highly stressful events in our lives. It is the most common of the depressive illnesses.

ENDOGENOUS DEPRESSION is a more rare type of depressive illness and is very much more to do with our biochemistry. It is called endogenous from the word 'endo' meaning inside. It can be serious and the feeling of black despair in these cases carries with it a huge risk of suicide. In the most severe cases it is as if there is a heavy damp blanket cutting out the sun, the warmth and all feeling. The ability to love, to laugh, to feel interest, to communicate, to enjoy food, to feel moved by anything, all goes. It is as if all information about the outside world has stopped. This is in fact exactly what happens.

It is now known that some of the brain chemicals which are involved in transmitting information between one nerve cell and another (the neurotransmitters) are altered in this type of depression. Their production is low. This, of course, affects all our function; the brain rhythms in sleep are altered, all sexual drive usually stops, appetite for food goes, and the storage of food is altered and weight often drops alarmingly.

If, on the other hand, there is an excess production of the chemicals, which can happen, then mania, the opposite of depression, occurs. People suffering from both swings are termed manic-depressives. This is now a condition easily treatable by Lithium Salts and your family doctor can easily arrange this.

■HANDLING DEPRESSION

Although the normal downs and the blues will come and go they need looking after, because at difficult and trying times – and we all have them – it is easy for those natural downs to depress our mood, stay longer than they should and cause us to slide into a real depression. The downs and the blues can occur when our systems are fighting infections, mopping up alien cells, dealing with alcohol, nicotine and other drugs and unwanted chemicals which we take in with food and drink. Therefore we can help our systems by:

1. Keeping the food we take in as pure and uncontaminated as we possibly can.
2. Leaving a week or two in between parties and entertaining when we are likely to eat, drink, and smoke more than we usually do.
3. Taking one gramme daily of vitamin C if feeling low. This is the anti-infective vitamin and helps the body to fight threatening infections.
4. Taking the vitamin B complex, including B12 (look at the contents carefully – B12 is called Cytocon); buy it separately but take all the B vitamins together as we need a balance of all of them in the body.
5. Developing a well-balanced life-style.

We think quite differently when we are depressed, have you noticed? 'It's no use', 'I can't do . . .', 'It won't work', 'It's no earthly use trying that'. It is as if we have a record of positives and negatives in our brain and the needle is stuck in the negative.

The positive approach will help you to lift the gloom. Here are three things to do:

1. Write down every negative thought and change it to a positive one.
2. Actively alter your appearance. Banish the sad slouch, regain your former life and smile whenever you pass the mirror.
3. Search for the happy emotions which you used to associate with the things you like. Warmth, affection, happiness and caring will come back as the emotional centres are stimulated, and the depression will quickly disappear. ●

JAMES: 'Right. Back to the article. Did you remember to note the date of the issue?'

DIGBY: 'Yes. It's not too old to be of value in theories on depression.'

JAMES: 'I presume you read the bold type below the title, the equivalent of the foreword in a book?'

DIGBY: 'I did.'

JAMES: 'And?'

DIGBY: 'It's about a certain doctor and the book she's written on causes and steps to take when feeling depressed.'

JAMES: 'So does this suggest anything to you?'

DIGBY: 'No, I don't think so. Why, is there something I should have noticed?'

JAMES: 'We'll take your word for the moment, so let's begin trailing the article. First I'll quickly run through it and number each paragraph, on pages 57 and 58, so that you can find each one easily as we discuss it.

Right! In the first paragraph I've joined the opening quotation with the next paragraph as number one. What does it tell you? Does it seem as if it will live up to its title?'

DIGBY: 'Yes. It intends to give "buck-up" advice of some sort.'

JAMES: 'I hope, by the way, that you didn't waste time reading the name of the doctor, the foundation etc. in this first paragraph. That's about one line out of six, more than 16 per cent, unnecessary to read. If you were so impressed at the end of the article that you wanted to remember the author's name, you could go back and make a note of it.

Paragraph two, what does the first sentence tell you?'

DIGBY: 'About the writer.'

JAMES: 'Important for your purpose?'

DIGBY: 'No.'

JAMES: 'Take a quick look through it to test.'

DIGBY: 'It does just tell you more about the writer.'

JAMES: 'Paragraph three tells you still more about her, unhappy marriage and so on. You don't need it.

There is one point made – 'Pamper yourself' . . . but you are only previewing and will miss the odd point.

Paragraph four is about her establishing a stress foundation. You don't need it for your purpose, which is. . ?'

DIGBY: 'To get advice to help your blues.'

JAMES: 'Paragraph four is about her stress foundation, which doesn't concern you.

Paragraph five is about her courses: don't need.

Paragraph six is a push to follow her advice. No advice given. If you check by reading the entire paragraph you'll see that.

Paragraph seven. The first sentence tells you she's on to her methods. You might need to read on, but you'll soon see nothing much in it for you.

Paragraph eight. First sentence tells you it's about depression: what it is. You want to help yours, not know about it, in this particular case that is.

Paragraph nine. At last she tells you there are ways of handling it yourself. Read it. Some advice is there.

Paragraph 10. She says in the first sentence she's going to give some advice. You would be reading it anyway as it is the last paragraph – it ends with a black circle which denotes an end. There's another section to the article (from the end of page 58 to the end of page 60), but we'll discuss that later.'

DIGBY: 'I can see how, by previewing, I saved time reading an entire article that hasn't fulfilled its promise so to speak. It doesn't live up to its title, the first section that is.'

JAMES: 'Ah! This is an interesting point and the reason I chose the piece. True, the title "What to do when you're feeling blue" seems to promise that, but the preface, or foreword, the blurb or whatever you call it below the title, as you mentioned hints that it's about Dr Booth and her foundation rather than a help-yourself guide. And when I asked if you'd taken note of all the important features in topping the article, in fact I think you did miss something. It does not say article by – Dr Booth in this case, the writer of the book on depression – but it is an interview with her by one of the magazine journalists. That alone suggests it's more about the author than what she said in her book. So, being active, topping it, would in fact have prepared you for all this and you should have expected an interview rather than self-help advice. Do you see my point?'

DIGBY: 'Oh yes, and it's a very valid one. I must be alert to all the bits and pieces involved in topping an article before I do more about it.'

JAMES: 'There are thus several important points illustrated here – the importance of topping an article well and trailing it. In short, it shows that previewing can save so much time and energy which would otherwise be wasted in reading what is not required.'

DIGBY: 'We haven't discussed the rest of the article (from the end of page 58 to page 60).'

JAMES: 'I'm coming to that. One presumes that these pages, though they don't actually say so, contain information taken from Dr Booth's book. Well here, by reading the headings alone, you can see quite clearly that they do, and what each section contains.

For a start, the author tells you how many kinds of depression there are. Should you be interested, though not as you set yourself for reading this piece, a quick look at the first sentence or part of each, will tell you what these are. For example, the chances are you wouldn't want to waste time reading the last paragraph in that section because you're not a woman. If, on the other hand, your wife suffers from depression you may want to look through it, but you would then be deviating from your purpose. In this instance it wouldn't matter, but in work situations, as in other aspects of your working life, you must not be distracted or sidetracked while on a specific job.

Getting back to the piece, note that only in the last section (pages 59 and 60), does the writer actually tell you how to handle depression.

So in summary, if you had only a minute or two

to see what you could get from the article, you could have found what you wanted pretty quickly.

Of course, if you'd looked through all the headings first, you could have found the significant section almost immediately, the answer to your purpose – how to handle your depression. How narrow your purpose is will determine how rigid your previewing is.

In a very short time you can establish whether or not the article lives up to its title, in which you were interested. I'll give you a copy of it and I suggest for your own interest that you take it home and read it through to confirm the value of previewing. You may learn a few more points of interest, but to read a whole article in the hope of picking up one or two points is a waste of time. On the whole, more is gained by reading several articles on any subject and taking the best each has to offer.

Later I'll show you how to skim articles, an extension of previewing, which will give you more information and fill out your previewing where necessary.

The value of previewing articles in work-related fields is inestimable. Most of us are faced with dozens of journals and magazines and we have to be ruthless.'

DIGBY: 'I see how I could have forged ahead with the XX project if I'd known how to tackle the mass of articles you gave me.'

JAMES: 'It was thoughtless of me to assume you'd know how to approach the mind-boggling list I gave you. The individual pieces appeared to be relevant, but then I was going by general subject-matter, or maybe title, and left the rest of the sifting for you. Now you'll know how to get started on it all.'

DIGBY: 'I'll do it right away.'

JAMES: 'And, by the way, you'll find the method very useful away from work, in hobbies and general interest reading. So much time is wasted by reading miles of print where so little is gained, either because the writer has in fact nothing of value to tell you, or because you know a lot about the subject and waste time reading material which tells you nothing new.'

DIGBY: 'In the same way, I suppose, I should preview the magazines and journals in which the articles are found.'

JAMES: 'Yes. The contents list is the skeleton for the book and will indicate what material will be covered. Think of it as a road map which gives you information beforehand and sets your course.

Then be rigid about marking or noting exactly which articles you will read. This is to avoid the temptation to read some for idle curiosity; you have a task ahead of you, stick to it.'

DIGBY: 'This all makes sense, but I still can't help feeling that sometimes it must be a waste of time previewing and then reading. For instance, if you've been given something to read and you're obliged to, whether or not it serves a purpose for you, why bother to preview?'

JAMES: 'It's been shown conclusively that a basic schema has to be formed only once and that can be done in the previewing, which extracts the gist of the article. Why look at a map before setting out on a journey, when you're going to travel the road yourself and see the signs along the way? If you're planning a trip across London, a quick look at the map will help you time it, let you know if you have to go through heavy traffic areas, or quiet suburbs.

Similarly, if you discover that one of the streets you regularly drive home through is being resurfaced, you reroute yourself, because you know in advance that you'll have problems if you don't.

So with reading. You can discover if the "journey" through the article or book is to be difficult or easy, if it's the right one for you to take, whether in fact to bother with it at all. You'll have discovered the likely trouble spots and can make the appropriate adjustments of reading speed more quickly. Likewise, when you know there are parts ahead which appear a waste of time you can prepare to jump over them. As when driving a car over humps, if you're familiar with them you can prepare for them, adjust your speed and travel smoothly on.

So, in summary, one can say that previewing gives you a general idea of the subject and the author's view so that you can decide whether or not it's worth reading. It gives you a chance to recall knowledge you already have which helps you relate to the new material. It gives you a taste of the vocabulary and style, so you're set to approach it correctly if you choose to go on with it. And, very important, it helps your concentration by pushing unrelated matter from your mind. You're "tuned in" to it.'

DIGBY: 'I suppose you could say that previewing, though done first, acts as a kind of summary of what you read later.

JAMES: 'I'm pleased you said that and it's reminded me to give you an excellent illustration of the importance of reading summaries as part of previewing whenever you come across them.

A study was carried out at one of the universities in the USA, where 1500 history students were given a long detailed chapter which they were required to read in a limited time so that there was the chance that they might not finish. At the end they were tested, firstly by multiple-choice questioning and, secondly, they had to write a short essay on the contents of the chapter. They also had to report on their method of approaching the assignment.

Over 90 per cent, as would be expected, began at page one of the chapter and proceeded to read it. They managed well enough on the multiple-choice questions, but when it came to the short concise essay, to show they'd understood the main message of the chapter, only a handful could give this short statement about it. They failed to understand the point of it. Yet there was a summary at the end of the chapter. If they had started with that it would have given them a clear picture of the piece. They became bogged down with the details, whereas they would have learned far more had they focused on the main points, all there for them at the end of the chapter. The writer had done their work for them in a way, and collected the key points in one passage. It also would have facilitated their reading afterwards, having given them the author's main thread and trend.'

DIGBY: 'You've convinced me. And apart from work I'm sure I'll find the method useful in my outside reading. I waste so much time reading articles from which I gain very little.'

JAMES: 'You should never waste time reading what you already know, or don't need. We'll end on that good piece of advice. See you next Wednesday.'

DIGBY: 'Right, and thanks.'

Summary

'3T Preview' all articles, i.e. *top, trail* and *tail* them:

Top – read title of article and magazine or journal. Note length of article, publication date and author. Note any brief foreword.

Trail – Read first paragraph. Read subheadings and the first sentence of each following paragraph.

Tail – Read last paragraph as you did the first.

Executive action

Preview three articles on a particular subject that interests you; articles that you would otherwise not have read. Select from your previewing the one you think is most worthwhile on the subject. Check if you have made the correct choice by reading all three.

Repeat the exercise on work-related articles.

6 Asking questions

JAMES: 'And how did the previewing of articles go?'

DIGBY: 'Very well. What a help! I went through them all, selected those that looked the best for the job and then, as it was the first time, I wanted to test the method. I put the articles in three piles, those which appeared best for me, those that might be suitable, and those that appeared least likely to contain what I needed. I then read a couple from each section and it worked admirably. From the first pile there was lots of information I could use, from the second only a few points, and from the third there was nothing I needed. I've discarded miles of print. My stack is down to a manageable size.'

JAMES: 'Sounds a very systematic way to test out. Well done. Keep at it. And now let's get on with the other questions you should ask as part of your active reading.'

DIGBY: 'I'm ready.'

JAMES: 'What are you reading at the moment, apart from work material?'

DIGBY: 'I've almost finished an interesting book. I decided to try some non-fiction. It's Bernard Levin's *Hannibal's Footsteps*.'

JAMES: 'What's it about?'

DIGBY: 'His journey, by foot, across part of France and over the Alps, following Hannibal's journey.'

JAMES: 'What's the theme?'

DIGBY: 'As I say, it's about his journey following Hannibal's.'

JAMES: 'That's a summary of the plot, if you like, the story. I want to know the theme, that is the author's purpose in writing it; what, if anything, lies behind the events. You should be able to sum it up neatly in a sentence or two – and everything you read. Remember our five questions? This is the second question you should ask after discovering your purpose for reading anything. What is the main theme of the book, or article? What is the point of it, what's the author up to, if you like? The writer has a specific theme in mind, or message to put across, both in fiction and non-fiction – apart from the most worthless material which we're not concerned with here – and you should be able to sum it concisely. So what is Bernard Levin telling you in *Hannibal's Footsteps?*'

DIGBY: 'Lots of things.'

JAMES: 'Yes, but there is always a main theme running through. As I said, every writer writes with a purpose, whether it's a book, article, letter; just as you the reader has one in reading it. You should always be on the lookout for the main thread, the leading theme. More than that, you must be able to state its essence in a sentence or two. It could simply be man against man, revenge, greed. You've just read *The Pearl*. What would you say is the theme, the main message of the book?'

DIGBY: 'I suppose greed, dishonesty and tragedy that follows as a result.'

JAMES: 'Fair enough. We won't go into it, but you can see that's a different answer from merely saying it's about a man who finds a great pearl and what happens to him as a result. I want you to find the theme as you read any book and follow it through.

So, what would you say is the theme of Bernard Levin's book? Is it merely a travel book?'

DIGBY: 'By no means. It says lots of things. I'm hard pressed to sum it up in a sentence or two. I suppose the theme is the challenge to the author of following in the footsteps of his great hero, encountering the varied landscapes which helped him to understand the magnitude of the difficulties involved in Hannibal's trek, and the changes in these areas and as they are today. I can see how trying to get at the heart of a book involves my being active, and having to think about it.'

JAMES: 'That's what I wanted you to realize. As for your summing up of the book, I can't comment as I haven't read it.'

DIGBY: 'But aren't some light novels, even better ones, simply a story and nothing more?'

JAMES: 'In those cases, no matter how long or complicated a book, there is one main story, the rest is episode; just as in non-fiction, there is one main message. Non-fiction, which is exposition, is informing you of something the writer wishes you to know about. He too has one main purpose, that will run through the book. Without unity, one theme, it becomes a collection of separate "booklets", not a single entity, and should be treated as such.

So now Digby, take that message home with you and be on the lookout for the main thread of a piece throughout your reading. It keeps you alert and gives you the point of the whole thing which you should bear in mind constantly.

But let's move on now, there are still three questions to be dealt with.

Remember question three? Ask yourself how the author or writer achieves the main theme, how he develops and structures his ideas.

It's impossible to cover this question other than very superficially as it involves the whole of analytical reading, which is beyond the scope of this mini-course. Of course you'd be aware of this if you have the theme or main purpose of these lessons firmly fixed in your mind.'

DIGBY: 'I'm not sure what you mean.'

JAMES: 'I'm merely suggesting that the aim of these sessions is to improve your reading in a practical way, so that you can cope with your work-related reading more efficiently, and also benefit more from your reading outside the office. My main purpose is not, therefore, to delve into analytical appreciation. If, within a dozen or so short sessions, I were to spend a disproportionate time discussing detailed construction of reading matter, you'd probably realize that this was out of place, not practising the aims of these short sessions.'

DIGBY: 'Yes, I see that would be a criticism of the course.'

JAMES: 'Exactly. We'll get onto the subject of criticism, in reading that is, a little later. But, returning to question 3 again, how the writer constructs his material, there are a few points that fit the scope of this discussion.

In writing, the writer starts with a theme, a skeleton, and covers it up artistically or logically depending on what he's aiming to achieve. You, the reader, must uncover it and be alert as to how the author fleshes out the bones. To do this you must understand the organization of the parts that make up the book. Any good book or article has an orderly arrangement of its parts. No matter how excellent the individual ideas in it, they must be put together carefully to make a satisfactory whole – just as a collection of the best ingredients lying on the kitchen table, flour, eggs, sugar etc. must be carefully "constructed", put together to make a delicious cake.

The structure of a book can completely change the way a basic idea comes across. There's a very different taste between scrambled and fried eggs, yet they're exactly the same constituents. They've just been differently structured.

It's as well to be aware of these things even if only at a superficial level. The more you are alert to the construction of a piece of reading matter, the better you'll concentrate, being actively involved in it. Your comprehension will improve and so will the value you get from what you read.

Take an example from the world of art. When I first learnt to look at positive and negative spaces in a painting, how much more interest it gave me the next time I visited an art gallery.'

JAMES: 'Sorry to sound so ignorant, but what are positive and negative spaces?'

JAMES: 'Ah! I thought you'd ask me. In a nutshell, the positive spaces are the actual objects or shapes being painted, while the negative shapes are those formed by the objects. In a well constructed painting the negative spaces are as important as the positive. In a Gauguin, for example, the spaces between the shapes of his Tahitian women form interesting shapes on their own. On a single canvas, all the surface is important. No artist of value will paint a scene and be concerned only with the actual objects in it. The whole surface must be one harmonious unit, all the parts are important. Knowing that can add an extra dimension to visiting an art gallery. You'll begin to notice at some of the local exhibitions that not all the contributors appear to take note of this.

The relevance of this to your reading is that, without doubt, the more you appreciate how things are developed, put together, the more benefit and satisfaction you'll derive from them. This applies in every aspect of life.'

DIGBY: 'Just one point though. You said in one of our earlier sessions how the details of a painting weren't important in order to get the feel of it – like the example with Van Gogh's sunflowers, how many there were and so on – yet aren't you now suggesting I should analyse it? Therefore, in reading, if I'm supposed to look out for structure – well, that's analysing.'

JAMES: 'I'm talking here of a general overview of the whole, not of particular detail as you go along. As you read you need an awareness of how the whole is structured. It doesn't have to slow you down, it should become part of your approach to reading. As I stressed before, it is your flexibility in reading speeds which is an essential element in efficient time management of your reading. Some books warrant more contemplation than others, and will take more time. Your approach, however, no matter what you are reading must be one of alertness and critical observation. That will tell you if it is worth reading even faster. So, with the structure of a book, if you find it has no coherence, no unity, no clarity, give it up and don't waste your time. You've a good reason for it. In the same way as you'd give up after one mouthful of a badly constructed, or baked, cake.

It's easier to illustrate my point with a work of fiction. In a well constructed novel, incidents making up the whole follow each other naturally, events are feasible within the scope and unity of it.

One of the reasons for the great success of Agatha Christie's detective stories is that all the evidence pointing to the culprit is there, hidden within the book. There are no sudden and unexplained events that don't tie in with the rest of the book. Imagine how cheated you'd feel if the murderer was introduced at the end of the book, with no evidence to lead you to work out the end. Your sense of probability would be outraged.

Weaknesses in structure do occur in great books, but this is unusual. *Wuthering Heights* by Emily Bronte is one of the greatest and most powerful love stories of all time but it has weaknesses and is, in part, clumsily constructed. This complicated story covering two generations lacks a certain unity between the two sets of characters and events, the first overshadowing the second. Nevertheless it remains an unforgettable and rereadable book.But this is an exception.'

DIGBY: 'It's interesting what you say. I agree that *Wuthering Heights* is a most powerful and moving book yet, though I couldn't put my finger on it, the second generation, the young Katherine for instance, is so insipid in a way compared to the main Katherine, that I did find it a let down. It lagged behind the power of the rest. Perhaps your having put words to my feelings, and if I had been on the lookout for it, I would have recognized what it was, and not blamed myself for wanting to get over those parts.'

JAMES: 'I'm pleased I've provided you with some food for thought over this. But we must get on. If you'd like to learn more about analytical reading, you can find shelves of books on the subject. And don't forget to preview well, to select the best for your purpose.

The next question you should ask yourself, after discovering the theme and being aware of how the author develops it, is "What is my criticism of the book or article I've just read?" '

DIGBY: 'Am I expected to criticize everything I read?'

JAMES: 'Yes.'

DIGBY: 'I find that difficult to accept. Surely there are some things I'll read, light material for sheer relaxation and entertainment, that don't justify criticism? My wife, for example, is a highly intelligent woman who enjoys reading lightweight mass-produced romances for relaxation. She gets through one in a couple of hours. I can't believe she needs to be alert and critical of them. They're all much the same with slight variations in plot and so on.'

JAMES: 'I'm not suggesting you need the same critical appraisal for these as for a well thought out novel. If you check with your wife, she'll tell you there are some romances that read better than others, hang together better; in some the use of language is superior, the story better constructed. If you're aware, you'd notice some characters for example don't ring true. Suppose an even-tempered man, in full control of his emotions and with very little provocation, were to bang his fist on the table, it would be out of character. Similarly, an amiable and sweet young girl is not likely to be rude and biting to her servants. A plot that relies solely on constant coincidences is badly constructed and, since there are literally thousands of these romances to choose from, I'm sure your wife, as the intelligent woman you say she is, must get more satisfaction from those higher quality, better constructed stories.

This applies to everything else, why not to reading? I'm sure she also appreciates a well made dress with a straight hem and seams that don't pucker – something my wife looks for in a garment.

When food is served attractively set out on a plate it's far more appetizing than when that same food is slopped all over it, swimming in gravy. Get the point?'

DIGBY: 'I do indeed.'

JAMES: 'Then don't you agree that you should be aware of how a piece of writing is constructed, how the writer clothes the skeleton of the book, artistically if it's a work of fiction, or logically if a work of exposition?'

DIGBY: 'I do.'

JAMES: 'Then in so doing you become critical of it, which brings us to question four: "What do I think of the book – what is my criticism of it?" '

DIGBY: 'So I'm obliged to find something wrong with everything I read?'

JAMES: 'It's amazing how the word criticism instantly brings to mind finding something wrong, whereas the *Shorter Oxford Dictionary* defines it "to pass judgement on the qualities" of anything. For our purposes it's the art of estimating the qualities and character of all written material.

Of course, a prerequisite for criticism is the need to have understood what you've read. You can't say a French book is good or bad if you don't understand French. But, seriously, no intelligent person should criticize anything without first being able to say, "I understand".'

DIGBY: 'But using the analogy to painting which you have at times, can't you say you like or dislike a painting without knowing necessarily what the artist is trying to tell you? And isn't it therefore similar with a book?'

JAMES: 'Ah, but as an intelligent reader of a book and viewer of a painting, you should be able to say *why* you like or dislike that book or painting. You can say a Matisse, for example, appeals to you because of its colour, the rhythm of its lines, but you must have reasons. Similarly you can say you don't enjoy looking at a Mondrian because you feel nothing from its few empty squares and three or four lines. *But* that is different from saying, as one hears in art galleries, "What rubbish, nothing in it, this isn't art", which shows the ignorance of the viewer rather

than the poor quality of the artist. If you can't understand a painting or a book, admit that to yourself,
and if you still wish to pass an opinion on it, at least
do so fully aware of the fact that maybe you don't
understand what it's trying to do. If you find in a
book that descriptions are tedious, the characters
unreal, the episodes unrelated to the whole – these
are valid criticisms. You've thought out your reasons
why you dislike something. But getting back to the
reading situation, let's take the problem of criticism
in an orderly fashion.'

DIGBY: 'A system for everything.'

JAMES: 'A systematic approach to all aspects of all skills
is a vital prerequisite.

Firstly, you must be critical, that is judge and
evaluate, assess everything you read. The writer has
said something and, as in any conversation, you owe
him the courtesy of observing an intellectual
etiquette, of answering him, as you would someone
in conversation. In talking to someone, you might
dismiss his case as nonsense or agree with him, but
you'd be expected to back up your opinions with
reasons. Similarly, you should feel obliged to do so
mentally with the written material you're reading.

The writer is trying to convince you, persuade you
to some story or idea, and you must react to it.
I repeat, whether you judge a book favourably or
unfavourably, you must be able to give reasons for
your opinion. That is the only active, intelligent and
rewarding way to criticize anything.

After all, you have reasons for all your thoughts
and actions. Taking a mundane analogy again, if
you don't eat a steak on your plate, you have a
reason; its too tough, too tasteless, too salty. If
there's nothing wrong with the steak, maybe the
reason is that you're a vegetarian or just not hungry.
Only a recalcitrant unreasonable child won't eat
something and offer no reason.

The intelligent reader is above that level of behaviour with his reading. If no reasons readily come to
mind why you think a book good or bad, then maybe
it's you, the reader, who needs to be criticized.

Perhaps you're prejudiced in favour of, or against, the topic.'

DIGBY: 'Isn't everyone prejudiced to some extent over most things?'

JAMES: 'Don't confuse prejudice with bias. Everyone is biased, that is, has come to a sincere conclusion on some issue, on the basis of background of experience or knowledge in the subject. But prejudice is very different. To be prejudiced is to hold opinions without any evidence to support them. Let's take a controversial issue like. . .'

DIGBY: 'Hanging.'

JAMES: 'Right. Well now, I have a friend who comes from a country where hanging is freely and often unjustly used, and therefore has very strong views against hanging. He is not prejudiced, for he recognizes this. He is very willing to listen to arguments in favour of hanging, and prepared, should he be faced with convincing evidence, to change his mind. That's the important difference. A biased person is prepared to be persuaded to change his mind, a prejudiced one is not.'

DIGBY: 'Like anti-abortionists who "know" it's wrong because they were brought up with it and just won't listen to any arguments in favour of it.'

JAMES: 'Yes indeed. Unfortunately too many people have closed minds. It's a good idea to read about different topics from different points of view. To read what you agree with is always easy, but it is essential to read the opposite opinions. And then you must be very wary of condemning the material, rather than yourself.

So in your criticism of what you read, be aware that you can criticize not only the text and the writer, but yourself, the reader.'

DIGBY: 'You're right. It's always much easier to find what's wrong with something outside of oneself. I must remember that.'

JAMES: 'Yet don't muddle giving reasons why something is to your taste with finding reasons for whether you think a work good or not. You must say "I like or dislike what you've written because. . .", as well as

"I think what you've written is good or bad because. . ." '

DIGBY: 'This all sounds very complicated and time consuming. Is it really necessary to do all this for everything I read?'

JAMES: 'Within limits, yes. The simpler the piece, the easier to criticize it; maybe only a second or two will be needed to give your opinion backed with reasons. But get into the habit of doing it if for no other reason than it'll keep you alert, your concentration high, because you're actively involved. Again, within the scope of this book we can't go into great detail about critical reading, but it's for you to be aware that you must judge, assess, everything you read, consciously.'

DIGBY: 'Is there a specific way to criticize?'

JAMES: 'It'll depend to some extent on whether you're judging fiction or non-fiction.'

DIGBY: 'How does that affect it?'

JAMES: 'We'll discuss fiction next week. As far as non-fiction, exposition, is concerned, that's the mainstream of work-related reading of course, there are three main critical positions. You can agree with it, disagree, or withhold judgement because you're unable to give an opinion due to not understanding, or because the arguments for example, are incomplete. If you disagree and criticize a book adversely, you must know exactly why you're condemning it. Does the writer appear to be uninformed, or misinformed or illogical? If you can't show why you disagree with a writer, you can't say you disagree with him. Again, look into yourself and your own prejudices.

Criticizing fiction has a different slant to it, and we'll talk about the differences in reading fiction and non-fiction next week. For the moment I'm trying to bring to your attention the need to be critical and to form opinions, to find reasons for them.

Remember that it's rare that any book is so bad that something good can't be found in it, or so good that no fault can be found. Quoting Sir Francis Bacon again: "Read not to contradict and confute, nor to believe and take for granted, nor to find talk and discourse, but to weigh and consider".

Before we close this subject of criticism though, I'd like to mention a couple of weaknesses prevalent in much that we read which you should note. Firstly, you need to recognize the difference between fact and opinion. This sounds obvious, but unfortunately most of us on occasion are taken in by statements claiming to be fact, but which, on analysis are based on opinion, unsubstantiated claims. In our daily reading of newspapers, magazines, political speeches, advertisements, the danger is always present and you must guard against it.

Tell me, the statement "bullfighting is barbaric," is that fact or opinion?'

DIGBY: 'Opinion.'

JAMES: 'You'd be surprised how many people are adamant that it's a fact.

"Women tend to be more intimate with each other, share themselves, than men." Fact or opinion?'

DIGBY: 'My wife certainly considers that a fact whatever the reasons, whereas I don't agree. I'd certainly say that's opinion, and in mine it's the behaviour style of an individual rather than their sex that makes them more closed or open with each other.'

JAMES: 'Say no more. My point is made. So many things we read and accept as fact can very possibly be opinion. Even Christopher Columbus's discovery of America is questioned by some historians. Though these were little catch questions, they embody the message that there's not necessarily a right or wrong answer to every question. You must recognize that what is stated as fact by a writer may well, on closer inspection, be seen to be opinion.'

DIGBY: 'Like listening to a clever politician.'

JAMES: 'Yes, or as in everyday slogans and advertisements such as "nine out of ten filmstars use. . .", or "doctors recommend. . ." Who are these filmstars, these doctors? Evidence of market research? We like to think we're immune to advertising, to simple slogans, but psychologists have shown how suscep-

tible we are. Don't take my word for it – there's
plenty of evidence to prove it.'

DIGBY: 'I realize that.'

JAMES: 'Good. And now, tied up with the whole question
of fact and opinion, and which is inherent in much
that we read, is propaganda. Only in rare situations
is the writer trying to convince you of something,
and often he uses techniques of propaganda to
achieve this. That is, he makes a deliberate attempt
to convert you to a particular viewpoint by playing
on the emotions, bypassing critical thought. You
must be aware of that.

One of the commonest techniques is the overuse
of loaded words, which is unacceptable in either
fiction or non-fiction, but in the latter it becomes
valueless. Too many superlatives hide weak
thinking on the part of the writer. Like the devalu-
ation of coinage, their power diminishes with
overuse. If too much is "dazzling, stupendous", these
words tend not to be taken seriously. Whether they
be "glittering generalities", rhetorical flourish, or
emotionally unpleasant, be aware of them. And, of
course, books that purport to teach, inform, give you
facts, but in reality are filled with opinions, unless
categorically stated as such are not worth reading,
so give them up.

Take, for example, this Second World War recruit-
ment poster in the USA. Private Joe Louis says:
"We're going to do our part . . . and we'll win because
we're on God's side. . ." We'll win? Who are "we"?
Does that refer to all the inhabitants of the US, all
the ethnic groups?

It's emotive to use the word "God" to suggest it's
good, it's right, but some people don't believe in God.
What does the comment actually mean?

You must watch out for all distortion, twisting,
half truths. Nowhere can you see that more clearly
than in the different arguments put forward by
political parties. They distort statistics and trade
figures to serve their purpose. You have to keep an
open mind, read both sides if you're to make a just
comment in the end.

I'm not suggesting you analyse and substantiate every statement you read, at times your purpose won't require it, but when it will influence you in your thinking it becomes important.

In general the need for a critical approach to your reading cannot be over-emphasized. You must be careful not to accept what you see in print, but critically evaluate it. Give neither indiscriminate praise nor wholesale condemnation of what you read in print. Unfortunately the printed word exercises a strange hold over us. Anything firmly stamped on paper tends to receive our respectful attention.

We must educate ourselves to examine every fact and every conclusion drawn from it we come across in print. As it was put so succinctly by J. Donald Adams: "An education, however conducted, that neglects the skeptical approach is no education at all. And if the wisdom of the world is in books, so, too, is a vast amount of nonsense".'

DIGBY: 'Who can argue with such wise words?'

JAMES: 'Indeed. And now let's take a quick look at our final question: What is the significance of what I've just read? When you finish reading anything, you should make some observation on it, continue your "intellectual etiquette" to a final judgement. What did you learn from it? Was it worth reading? Did it fulfil your purpose and expectation in reading it? Did the writer appear to have fulfilled his purpose in writing it?

For example, take again the article we previewed on what to do when you're feeling blue. Did it fulfil its purpose for you?'

DIGBY: 'Not really, but possibly that was because I'd made the mistake of expecting what was not offered. It was first and foremost an interview with the author of the book on how to help your depression.'

JAMES: 'Which, as we said earlier, you could have deduced from the blurb alongside the title. Was the article then worth the reading? But let's not go on with that particular article. The point is that you should consider, no matter how briefly, the significance of what you've just read.'

DIGBY: 'I see the sense in that.'

JAMES: 'Well, that covers briefly the five questions you must ask of all your reading material. Get into the habit of asking them. Expand or contract them as the material warrants. Read on the subject to develop more fully in this direction. I'm only able to open your eyes and show you what road to take.

DIGBY: 'So these questions cover all you need to ask of a book?'

JAMES: 'Yes, they summarize the whole obligation of you, the reader. Read actively by questioning and you'll channel your concentration into what you're reading, and improve your comprehension.

By making demands on yourself and of the material, you'll become more discerning in all your reading and therefore learn more from it. Many books may be dull, but the unquestioning reader is duller. Don't allow yourself to become one of those.

Samuel Johnson once said: "What is written without effort is in general read without pleasure." I'd like to add a corollary to that: "What is read without effort is in general read without pleasure". It's the same old adage, the more you put into your life, your work, your leisure, your reading, the more you get out of it.

We'll leave off at this point till next week.'

DIGBY: 'Thank you James, see you next week.'

Summary

Further questions to ask yourself of your reading are:

Question 2   What is the main theme or point of the book?

Question 3   How does the writer achieve this, how does he develop his main ideas?

Question 4   What is my criticism of the book?

Question 5   What is the significance of the book?

Executive action

Take up a book or article and ask yourself all the above four questions, having first asked your purpose, which involves previewing.

Make a particular point of imagining you are having a conversation with the writer of what you are reading and talk back to him or her.

7 Fiction and non-fiction

JAMES: 'Ah Digby, so now let's see, where are we in our reading programme?'

DIGBY: 'We've been discussing the active role I should play in my reading by asking questions.'

JAMES: 'And have you been doing this over the past week?'

DIGBY: 'I've tried.'

JAMES: 'You don't sound too happy about it.'

DIGBY: 'It's a whole new orientation for me.'

JAMES: 'Everything takes getting used to. Reprogramming is always difficult, but you'll find it pays in the end.'

DIGBY: 'I can't deny that. Taking the question of finding the theme in a book – it's very interesting. It really makes you think about a book to express the gist of it in a sentence or two. I don't get so bored in my reading as I used to. Going faster helps of course, plus reading with a purpose.'

JAMES: 'Good to hear it. A far cry from my first encounter with you over your reading.'

DIGBY: 'As I say, I feel quite differently about it. I think it's the confidence I'm building in my ability that's a most important asset, also the correct approach and using systematic methods, which I still have to work at mind you – concentrating at times on overcoming the barriers to speed and pushing myself on, but I'm finding that easier as time goes on.'

JAMES: 'But you're remembering not to read everything at the same speed I hope?'

DIGBY: 'Yes, I'm far more flexible than I ever was. When something's easy reading, I just know I can go faster and do. And I vary my speed according to what, or how much, I want from a particular read.

The strange thing is that although I'm going faster, I'm aware that I'm picking up extra bits of information I'd never have in the early days. I leave out what I know or have anticipated or what's not important, and find time for new things.'

JAMES: 'And I suppose being supplied with more and more information makes you feel good, satisfies you?'

DIGBY: 'What are you getting at?'

JAMES: 'I mean, do you feel that the principal value of reading is to gain information, knowledge?'

DIGBY: 'Well isn't it?'

JAMES: 'By no means. You should read in order to acquire knowledge certainly, but there's another equally valuable facet to reading, how should I say it, reading "for life". After all, during our life span only a limited amount can be experienced so the only way we can enlarge the scope of our own life beyond what we can live, is through the experiences of others, even fictional characters.

Langdon Smith perhaps went a little far when he maintained that whereas people said that life was the thing, he preferred reading, but certainly, experience through reading can lead to a fuller life. It helps develop and broaden horizons and can often change values and attitudes to life.'

DIGBY: 'Isn't that, in a sense, through information? If you read about Scott of the Antarctic and his experiences, you're gaining information, learning about his life experience.'

JAMES: 'Ah, but do you really experience those experiences?'

DIGBY: 'No, of course not. They're Scott's experiences, not mine, but you said we can live through reading.'

JAMES: 'Let me explain more fully. Non-fiction, expository writing, is a form of communication of information. It tells you about someone or something; it instructs, teaches you, if you like. It doesn't attempt to recreate the experience for you, involve you as fiction does where you are expected to identify, live in the set scene. Without fiction it's unlikely that the feminist ideology could have taken hold so rapidly. Even the simplest feminist fiction has been known to influence many women, waking them up to the injustices of a male-dominated society.

It's not surprising, therefore, that totalitarian governments ban so much literature which is a permanent threat to the state's rigid ideas, by influencing their citizens with new ones contrary to those the state wishes to perpetuate. About a year ago I read in the newspaper of a middle-eastern country where husbands who taught their wives to read and write were punished severely, for that very reason no doubt.'

DIGBY: 'You stress these changes brought about by reading fiction. Is this really so?'

JAMES: 'Yes, it is largely through fiction that one experiences, and imaginative literature is therefore far more potent than when one is simply told about something. In fiction you can become more fully involved and subtly changed. But unfortunately not everyone is aware of the value of reading for life experience through reading fiction. Too many people are guilty of this. Some even consider reading good fiction as a waste of time, impractical, unrelated to life or their work and therefore pointless.

Underestimating the value of fiction is nothing new. It was certainly frowned upon for young ladies to read novels in the eighteenth century. To quote from Jane Austen's *Northanger Abbey*:

> "And what are you reading, Miss –?" "Oh! it is only a novel," replies the young lady while she lays down her book with affected indifference, or momentary shame.

Unfortunately in some quarters that attitude still exists today.

Only the other day I was listening to a chat show host interviewing one of our top actors, also a writer and a painter, and when asked what book, his second, he was busy writing, he replied, "It's a novel, I'm afraid to confess." No doubt he meant nothing by it, but by implication it's almost as if he felt it was a little shameful.'

DIGBY: 'Isn't it more a case today of people being too involved with their jobs and then having other forms of entertainment? It's much easier to watch television.'

JAMES: 'This does play a role, but there are still some people who actively declaim against fiction as a waste of time. Some individuals consider it "highbrow", pretentious. I've read of men who say it is even effeminate to read worthwhile literature. If only they'd consider at least the practical advantages of reading good fiction, apart from the joy for those who appreciate it.'

DIGBY: 'What are the practical advantages?'

JAMES: 'Without a doubt, reading worthwhile literature exposes one to proficiency in the use of language which leads directly to one's own proficiency and thus to better communication with others. In the same way that you pick up the accent and idiom of those you grow up with, so you can develop excellence in a language through a thorough grounding in the output of good writers. I'd go further, in fact, and say that you cannot be proficient in the use of language without a broad background of reading experience. Bad spelling and a poor expression when writing are further deficiencies resulting from a limited reading'.

DIGBY: 'Come to think of it, the people I meet who are most erudite are generally widely read.'

JAMES: 'To be well-read is more important than to be widely read. But, as I've already said, it's in the subtler aspect of developing yourself that the main value of fiction reading lies. It helps develop your own personal and social values, and can even help solve your problems. Because "good" fiction deals with the basic human problems and conflicts in human beings, and their resolution, this helps readers to reflect on their own conflicts and to deal with and perhaps resolve them. Insensitivity to language leads to insensitivity to the quality of life.'

DIGBY: 'How, exactly, do you see reading literature develops personal and social values?'

JAMES: 'Human values develop in society through inter-action with other people, by identifying with them, modelling behaviour on some, inspired by others and so on. The power invested in a good writer enables an individual to do the same with imaginary charac-ters, often more potently, the reader becoming for a while wholly involved with them.

History is full of people who claim to have made decisive changes in their lives, even revalued them completely, as a direct result of the effect on them of strongly developed imaginary characters in literature.

Young people particularly are often swayed and influenced more by a novel or a play on an important social issue, say drugs, than by a documentary informing them of the subject.

I recall reading a particular study of young people. One girl, commenting on the book *Karen*, by Killilea, said how after reading it she tried harder at the things she did, because of the way the heroine in the book fought against such odds and how little *she'd* had to fight for. Another maintained that reading *The Cross and the Switchblade*, by Wilkinson, inspired her to do charity work at a camp for young people. The book *Black Like Me* changed the attitude of dozens of youngsters allowing them to "live" with the racial situation so that their attitude underwent change.

People's desire to share experiences can often be satisfied by sharing the same desires, problems and so on with fictional characters.'

DIGBY: 'What you're saying makes such sense, though before now I'd never thought much about it. But why is it we're so lacking in an awareness of the personal and practical advantages of reading literature?'

JAMES: 'I think it's largely the fault of an education which often fails in its approach to literary works. We're rarely given any convincing reasons for reading good literature, or told what it can do for us. Young people, particularly those who are keen to get on in the world, need to be shown the value to themselves, in all aspects of reading, just as they are shown the value of learning the computer.

An interesting experiment was carried out by the Bell Telephone Company in the USA in 1954, when a group of businessmen were selected over a ten-month period at the University of Pennsylvania. It arose from a complaint at the very top of the company that too many of its executives, while experts in their field, were not broadly educated. It was felt that a wider approach to education might add that extra dimension to their ability and range of intelligent application to their work.

They were thrust, as it were, into the field of the imagination – of the arts, the humanities, as opposed to the sciences. Apart from visits and courses on the fine arts and music, they were required to read worthy works of literature, often quite foreign to what they were used to, and often difficult to understand. This was all directed to stimulating their intellect in new directions.

The whole exercise had quite a profound effect on the men which may well last their lifetime. They all felt that they had been introduced to new worlds of ideas, values and interests, and many of them claimed to have changed quite radically. They made comments such as "learning about themselves", "feeling whole" and "gaining self confidence". Certainly their reading became much wider, their approach more speculative and contemplative.

So always remember that reading is basic to our education in its broadest sense in two ways, giving us knowledge, and giving us "life".'

DIGBY: 'I've always felt I'm lacking, missing some dimension in my life by not having had this very broad, liberal arts education, and I'm especially aware of what I've missed by reading so little worthwhile literature. Now I feel more competent to cope with it I intend making a start, but I'd like to know how to approach fiction reading. You did say we'd discuss it this week.'

JAMES: 'Yes. There *is* a difference of approach between fiction and non-fiction because there's a basic difference in purpose, both for the writer and the reader.'

DIGBY: 'What is this difference?'

JAMES: 'As I've already suggested, the main purpose of exposition is to give the reader knowledge, information of some sort or another. The purpose of imaginary literature is to give the reader the experience rather than just tell about it. In this sense the reader only learns derivatively.

From the reader's point of view, a novel is read for enjoyment, it's valueless otherwise. Its aim is to please. There's no obligation to read fiction, apart from student reading, and therefore it's read as a diversion not as a task. All art form aims to please. This is generally accepted by writers, artists and philosophers – to entertain, in its broadest sense.'

DIGBY: 'And how does your different purpose affect your actual reading?'

JAMES: 'In fiction, you need, from the start, to make yourself open to the experiences the author is aiming to give you. He or she is creating a world for you to live in, and you must make yourself part of it. Your goal in reading fiction is to have as profound an experience as possible, to get the most "life experience" from it. To achieve this, the reader must give something of himself, the writer has a right to demand it – an interest in his characters and their affairs. Then he can gain the most the novel has to offer.'

DIGBY: 'But when I read *Scott of the Antarctic*, I still feel I read it to experience what he did, as I do a character in fiction.'

JAMES: 'You're not expected to be in the action, but to understand it. You're looking down on it, a bird of prey over it, rather than being part of it. It is informing you of things, events, feelings, and therefore you read it from a different point of view.

In literature the emotions are involved. You're

rather more subjectively than objectively involved as with non-fiction, no longer a bird of prey.'

DIGBY: 'But surely you should still be critical, alert, judging?'

JAMES: 'Yes, but in a different way. Take the language, for instance. In exposition, because it's communicating information, it must be unambiguous, clear, explicit, logical, have no inconsistencies, no fallacious arguments. Those are the things you look for.

In fiction, however, the very richness of the language is imparted through creative ambiguity, metaphor, through reading between the lines. You only have to think of Shakespeare's plays and the endless discussion of what exactly a certain line means, or tells you about a character. This would be entirely out of place in an "informing" piece of writing, where you should put aside anything that is ambiguous. To be satisfactory the language must be clear and exact. You are looking for the truth of what is said.

In fiction you're looking for a different kind of truth, rather a verisimilitude, the air of truth. The writer wants you to believe that what he tells you is actually happening. In this sense, by dramatizing, he arranges his facts to capture and hold your attention, sacrificing truth as it is used in scientific or other informative works. He can create whatever bizarre world he likes, but it must be plausible in terms of how it is created.

Briefly what you should look for in a good novel is a widely encompassing theme of human and enduring interest. Also the story must be coherent and persuasive, each event a natural consequence of what went before, so that all episodes develop and grow out of the story.

And, of course, the characters must ring true within their world. They must speak and act in character. An uneducated stable boy can't converse in the same manner as a highly educated gentleman, to take a simple example. These are the sorts of judgement you should make. As a start then you must be aware that fiction and non-fiction are different forms of writing, and therefore need different approaches when reading.'

DIGBY: 'Being a critical reader of fiction sounds more difficult.'

JAMES: 'It is. It's always more difficult reading an art form. An Aristotle said: "Beauty is harder to analyse than truth". Reading exposition is concerned with factual material, and it's easier to say why you do or don't agree with the writer, than it is to say why you like or dislike a novel.'

DIGBY: 'Another thought comes to mind, the speed of reading fiction. I see that so long as I understand what a writer is saying in non-fiction I can go as fast as I'm able, but in fiction, surely I should read beautifully written prose more slowly to appreciate the language? Is the style of a writer not lost in a worthwhile piece of fiction by reading it fast?'

JAMES: 'What *is* style in writing? What makes one author use one style, another a different style?'

DIGBY: 'It's the writer's way of putting over what he or she wants to say.'

JAMES: 'Exactly. A writer's style paints the picture to put across his message. He uses language to get somewhere. That is, his or her aim is to impart something, not to use words for their own sake, which sounds awfully contrived when it's attempted by a phony writer. The better the style, the more readable, and therefore you should be able to read it faster than a badly written piece in poor style. No matter how poetic prose is, it is prose and should be read as such, for what is being unfolded – thoughts, action, atmosphere and so on. Word order and rhythm plays a more important role in poetry proper, or in plays where the sound of words is important. Some authors' prose has the great quality of "ear", and in fact is good to read aloud, but that's the exception. Even in poetry, the meaning and rhythms can often be lost by too slow a reading. Rather read through a poem several times fast than once too slowly. If, after reading and emotionally reacting to a poem you should wish to analyse it, that's a different matter. But first you must react to it, make yourself open to its effect.

Let's return to the painting analogy. You can't start by analysing colour, positive and negative space, shapes and so on in a Matisse. First you must let it have its impact on you.

In much the same way in our lives, we live them, react to situations, events. We can't sit back and analyse everything as we live it or we wouldn't be able to live. We can only do that after an event.

But to return to writing and style, let me read you this quotation by H. G. Wells: "I write as I walk because I want to get somewhere and I write as straight as I can, just as I walk as straight as I can, because that is the best way to get there". Reading for his meaning should be "easy" in the light of this.'

DIGBY: 'But in some excellent prose the images are more complex, more profound, and involve more contemplation in receiving the message.'

JAMES: 'True. You can't read everything equally fast, as I've said before. Obviously the more complicated the message or the thinking of a passage, the slower you will need to go to understand it, but that's because the thoughts are complicated, not because the writing is difficult, being "good". But again, it's better to read through something twice at a faster rate than analyse as you go through imaginative fiction. As with life – live it, analyse afterwards if necessary. Excellent prose does not, by virtue of that quality, automatically require slower reading. It should rather encourage smooth and efficient reading.

Jane Austen's well-known opening words in *Pride and Prejudice*, "It is a truth universally acknowledged, that a single man in possession of a good fortune, must be in want of a wife" . . . is glorious, but it's easy to read and understand.'

DIGBY: 'But some books, fiction or non-fiction, *are* difficult to read.'

JAMES: 'Most definitely. I repeat, the nature of the writing must influence your reading speed. "Worthy" prose, shall we call it, does not necessarily involve slow reading. Bad writing certainly does: it's difficult to fathom, convoluted, unclear.

Talking of difficult books, here's some good advice about reading them.'

DIGBY: 'Any advice in that direction would be most welcome. I still do worry and become anxious when I can't fully understand what I'm reading.'

JAMES: 'And then you fall into the trap of becoming over conscientious in tackling it, worrying about every word, sentence and paragraph?'

DIGBY: 'It's difficult not to.'

JAMES: 'What you must learn to do when tackling any difficult book for the first time is to read it straight through, not stopping to ponder what you don't understand right away. Pay attention to what you do understand. If you read straight through, you'll find there's enough for you to grasp. You'll read past the point where you have difficulties in understanding.'

DIGBY: 'But then you're probably missing a lot that's important and reading very superficially.'

JAMES: 'It may appear like that, but it's the best way, the only way, to read before trying to comprehend. In the end, if you never reread it to understand it more fully, understanding and retaining only 50 per cent of a truly worthwhile book is of more value than 100 per cent of a worthless one from which you learn nothing.

Take, for example, one book generally avoided by the reading public – Plato's *Republic*. If, as a novice, you try to understand everything on the page, you're very likely to give up in despair early on. But it's open to the layperson if approached correctly. You would be able to understand the essence of what the great man says.'

DIGBY: 'I must say I do feel guilty about what I miss when I read a difficult book.'

JAMES: 'Worthwhile books, like worthwhile people, can be close friends or passing acquaintances, and you can derive benefit from both in their own way. You don't have to know a person intimately in order to admire him or her. You can derive benefit from whatever little access you have to that person's words or deeds. Similarly you may derive benefit from some books, though you'll never understand or take in everything.

Unfortunately we've been taught since early school days to concentrate our attention on what we don't understand, pausing over sentences that puzzle us rather than those that interest us. The average teaching of Shakespeare is a good example. The entire text is rarely read through in one go, but each line is discussed and analysed as it is reached. Is it any wonder this becomes uninspiring, boring, the child losing the wood for the trees? Yet, I can recall watching my son at the age of eight enjoying a well-produced *Twelfth Night* at Stratford-upon-Avon; laughing, getting the gist of it, its feel and something of its value.

Analysing everything as you go along will impede your reading instead of helping it. It'll probably force you to give up the book early on in your reading and then you'll not be reading well on any level.'

DIGBY: 'I suppose at least that way you'll give a difficult book a good chance and get well into it before deciding to give it up for reasons other than its difficulty.'

JAMES: 'Yes, and you may be pleasantly surprised because, as a general rule, difficult books usually become more specific as they progress and therefore easier to understand. The first chapters tend to be more abstract in the case of non-fiction, as the main ideas and concepts are developed, and in fiction, unfamiliar scenes and characters are introduced.

So remember, in first approaching any difficult material, read straight through, hurdle over the difficult parts and continue concentrating on what you do understand.'

DIGBY: 'That strikes me as very useful advice which, as you say, applies equally to fiction and non-fiction. I'll have to try it out on some of those *Harvard Business Review* articles I had in mind when I said I worried about difficult pieces.'

JAMES: 'And don't forget to try it out with some difficult worthwhile fiction as well.'

DIGBY: 'Will do. But there's one other point here. I often find when I've attempted to read some of the great Russian writers particularly that I get hopelessly muddled with the characters. I have to keep turning back to work out who's who and invariably I give up. Won't reading straight through make matters worse? How can I ever catch up on all the characters?'

JAMES: 'Tell me, when you first started this job and were introduced to the staff, did you remember who each individual was and their role in the organization?'

DIGBY: 'No, can't say I did. Took me a while to get it all sorted out.'

JAMES: 'When you go to a party and meet people, do you remember who's who always?'

DIGBY: 'Only those who stand out in the crowd, for me that is.'

JAMES: 'Exactly. So it is with fiction. The writer will make sure that the main characters stand out in the crowd. Gradually they'll emerge as important, while others remain only as the crowd, forming the atmosphere, the background, much like the crowd scenes in a film, backing the main character. Don't worry, the author will flag the important characters as time goes by. As in life, you can often only understand events as they occur with the passage of time, similarly with events in imaginary time.'

DIGBY: 'That all sounds very reassuring. Seems a reader certainly needs to know what he's doing.'

JAMES: 'As much as the writer does. As Ralph Waldo Emerson said: "Tis the good reader that makes the good book".

And at this point I think we'll call it a day. Though it's been a very general discussion I hope it's put some new thoughts into your mind to mull over. At least it'll encourage you to tackle more worthwhile and difficult reading, both fiction and non-fiction, and thereby broaden yourself generally. And if it seems that I've talked a lot about fiction, when I said in the beginning I was only concerned with your work-related reading, it's because they cannot be separated. Each complements the other. In order to expand you need both reading for knowledge, and reading for life; as I think the Bell Telephone Company experiment showed.'

DIGBY: 'I agree, and thanks. I've enjoyed this discussion.'

JAMES: 'Before you go, let me ask you about your reading speed. Do you still test yourself periodically?'

DIGBY: 'Yes I do. I've stabilized at a higher speed.'

JAMES: 'I'm pleased you mentioned the stabilizing factor. You now know you can never read everything, or even the same book every time you pick it up, at the same rate, but the point is that as you improve your skills, your average will stabilize at a higher level than your original speed. In fact, what I'd like you to do now is to take out your novel. Do you have it?'

DIGBY: 'Yes.'

JAMES: 'I want you to start reading at a particular point – mark it – and read for two minutes. I'll time you. Read very slowly, at the speed you first tested yourself. Read how you feel you read then. Do you remember the speed you first tested at?'

DIGBY: 'About 200 words per minute.'

JAMES: 'Right' [taking out his stop watch] 'when I say begin do so, and remember I want you to read the way you feel you were reading then, about 200 words per minute.'

[Digby reads for two minutes.]

JAMES: 'Stop. Now calculate your speed.'

DIGBY: 'About 300.'

JAMES: 'But I told you to read as slowly as when you began this course.'

DIGBY: 'I was, I'm sure. I felt I really was reading every word. I found it an effort and I kept wanting to go faster.'

JAMES: 'Well, there you are. You'll find you're not able to go back to your original ways once you've improved your reading skills.'

DIGBY: 'I really find that most encouraging, to see such evidence of my improvement.'

JAMES: 'Once you've settled into the routine with your

reading, like a tennis or golf swing, small faults might creep in, so you should be on guard, but you'll never go back to the old clumsy ways.

Now we must call it a day. See you next week.'
DIGBY: 'Thanks again. See you next week.'

Summary

1 The value of reading is twofold:
  (a) To acquire knowledge;
  (b) to read 'for life' – enlarge one's life experience.
2 There is value in reading imaginative literature:
  (a) it helps develop personal, social values, solve personal problems, broaden horizons;
  (b) it leads to proficiency in the use of language and therefore communication.
3 Advice on reading difficult books:
  (a) Read past difficult parts and concentrate first time round on what you do understand;
  (b) don't be deterred by lots of characters in a book, the important ones will emerge from the crowd as you read on.
4 As far as speed is concerned, you will find you are uncomfortable going back to your earliest speeds.

Executive action

Select one worthwhile piece of literature you would hitherto have felt too difficult or slow a read and, armed with the above advice, read it and reflect afterwards on what you feel you've learned from it in the light of all that's been discussed so far.

Try reading very slowly, as you felt you read when you started on this programme. Then speed up again, and notice how much more comfortable you feel.

8 Skimming

DIGBY: 'I shall become truly educated, in the widest sense I mean, with all this advice you've given me.'

JAMES: 'What's prompted that prediction?'

DIGBY: 'I'm in the middle of reading *A Portrait of The Artist As a Young Man*, which I guess is considered by most to be a worthwhile read, and enjoying it. I did what you said, went faster in the beginning to get past the opening chapter which I did find tedious. I also skipped some bits here and there, yet I've certainly got the atmosphere, the ambience of the book, the ideas, the feeling of the characters and so on. While I'm sure I'm by no means taking it all in, I believe I'm also benefiting enormously.'

JAMES: 'So you're feeling pleased with yourself, are you?'

DIGBY: 'In this respect yes, but there's an awful lot for XX waiting to be read, which haunts me. So far I've previewed it and reduced the amount I now have to read, but that still has to be done.'

JAMES: 'Not to worry. We're going to take our previewing a stage further and I'm going to show you how to skim correctly, that will help you to get through most of the articles.'

DIGBY: 'But isn't skimming the same as going quickly, skipping parts and looking for only the things I need, which I'm already doing?'

JAMES: 'Skimming is more than a haphazard speeding up and skipping here and there. As I think I mentioned before, it involves using specific techniques for a specific purpose. While it can't take the place of reading, it provides another "gear" to use. It's essential for any business executive like yourself to be able to skim effectively. You can't cope well without it.

As Earl Balfour said: "He has only half learnt the art of reading who has not added to it the more refined accomplishments of skipping and skimming". Gilbert carried it even further when he said: "The art of reading is to skip judiciously".'

DIGBY: 'I do skip parts of what I'm reading.'

JAMES: 'Everybody does to some extent, but to do so without loss isn't easy, as Somerset Maugham suggested. As far as fiction is concerned, you learn to judge when and what to skip to suit yourself. For non-fiction certainly, you should have a preconceived plan of action for your skimming.'

DIGBY: 'Which I don't have.'

JAMES: 'Everything you do regarding your reading – as with the time management of all aspects of your job – for maximum efficiency, you must order, plan, know what you're doing, when and why.'

DIGBY: 'From what I've learnt already I accept that. So what exactly is skimming?'

JAMES: 'Skimming "takes the cream off the top". It aims to find out the specific information you require, by discarding irrelevant material as your eyes move down the page and purposely leaving out whole chunks. It involves a different type of comprehension to reading per se. It's an inspectional rather than an analytical reading.

It's a process built up in stages. Firstly, you must select the area where you're to find the facts you seek, then you skip vast sections within that to locate where you're likely to find them and finally you look closely to extract the exact details you want. A simple illustration of this process is using a telephone directory. You select the correct volume; you skip pages till you come to the required capital letter of the name you want; you skim down the pages as you approach the letters of the alphabet that make up the name, and finally you scan, that is look closely for the details of the person, the initials and then the address.'

DIGBY: 'That's easy enough. You know exactly what you want, and exactly where to find it.'

JAMES: 'It's like visiting your local supermarket or library, with which you're familiar. You can go straight to the appropriate aisle for a particular brand of tinned soup, or to the exact shelf for your book on management or travel.

The next stage up from that becomes a little more difficult, when you know what information you want but you're not sure where to find it. Even at this early stage most people start to go wrong. They tend to read on passively, waiting till the portion they want takes its turn in sequence for their eyes to find it out.

And that's inefficient, wasteful of time and energy. You'd never enter a new supermarket wanting a tin of Heinz's tomato soup, and walk up and down every aisle searching all the shelves along the way for it. Nor would you look along all the shelves in your library for a volume on business management in Japan. How would you set about finding your tin of soup in a supermarket?'

DIGBY: 'Look out for labels, signposts above the shelves.'

JAMES: 'And if you were in a Japanese supermarket and didn't speak the lingo?'

DIGBY: 'Look for other identifying signs I suppose, like rows of tins, whether they've pictures of fruit or vegetables on them.'

JAMES: 'Yes, your eyes would skip right over the freezers, the rows of flour and sugar bags. They'd only pause as you found tins with steaming soup bowls, and the like. Correct?'

DIGBY: 'Correct.'

JAMES: 'It's the same with reading. Too few people apply the same principles, actively searching out what they want rather than glossing aimlessly over all the material in the hopes of finding it.

Let me illustrate with example. I'll take a volume of *The World Book Encyclopedia* off the shelf, turn to any page. Right here, [places open volume in front

of Digby] 'the insertion on Wills, Helen Newington.
Point to the part that tells you in what year she won
Wimbledon.'

WILLS, HELEN NEWINGTON (1906–　　), won
more major tennis championships than any other
woman in the world. She won the United States
women's title seven times. She was noted for her ability
to hit the ball harder than any woman she faced and
for poise that earned her the name "Little Miss Poker
Face." She won her first US women's tournament in
1923, and retired after winning at Wimbledon in 1938.
She was born in Centerville, Calif. After marrying
Frederick Moody in 1929, she played as Helen Wills
Moody.　　PAT HARMON*

[Digby finds and points to the answer.]

'Judging from the time you took I'd say you looked
over the entire piece till you came to the answer.'

DIGBY: 'Very summarily.'

JAMES: 'No preconceived plan of finding the answer then,
I gather?'

DIGBY: 'No.'

JAMES: 'Isn't there anything you could have used as a
pointer to the answer, a label when looking for a
date?'

DIGBY: 'Numbers I suppose. . .'

JAMES: 'Quite! Then your eyes need literally have
blurred over almost the entire piece till the numbers
pop out at you – first 1923 they'd pause over, then,
seeing this was wrong, on to the next, 1938 which
gives you the answer. Just the very act of setting
your purpose to find numbers would speed up your
finding the answer.

Now in this piece on Horace Walpole, what was
his most influential literary work?'

Horace Walpole (1717–1797), the youngest son of the
prime minister, was a letter writer, author, and art
lover. Even at a time when personal letters were

---

* From *The World Book Encyclopedia*, © 1988 World Book, Inc.,
Chicago.

considered a minor art form, Walpole's huge correspondence is remarkable. His witty letters provide an entertaining documentary of life in English high society. They report social and political gossip, and express Walpole's opinions on literature and the arts.

As a scholar fascinated by medieval life, Walpole greatly influenced the Gothic revival of the late 1700's. He transformed Strawberry Hill, his house in Twickenham, into a miniature Gothic castle. He built a printing press nearby, and published many of his own writings. His most influential literary work is *The Castle of Otranto* (1764). This tale of terror and the supernatural was the first of what became known as Gothic novels.

Walpole was born in London. He served in Parliament from 1741 to 1768. In 1791, he succeeded to the family title as the fourth Earl of Orford.

MARTIN C. BATTESTIN*

DIGBY: [Almost immediately] '*The Castle of Otranto.*'

JAMES: 'Good, that was quick. Plan your searching this time?'

DIGBY: 'Indeed. I looked only for italics and the answer was right there.'

JAMES: 'And if you were looking for the name of a person, a town, what would you look for?'

DIGBY: 'Capital letters.'

JAMES: 'Remember that. Now in this entry on the Walrus, using the same principle and a conscious plan, how would you find out what is the walrus's favourite food?'

DIGBY: 'Look for the key words, favourite food, and read only when you see that.'

WALRUS is a sea animal that lives in parts of the Arctic, North Atlantic, and North Pacific oceans. It has two ivory tusks, and its four feet are flattened into flippers. The flippers make the walrus a good swimmer.

During the winter and spring, walruses drift along on large floating fields of ice. In summer, some may

* From *The World Book Encyclopedia*, © 1988 World Book, Inc., Chicago.

rest on shore. A walrus spends much time in the water searching for clams, its favourite food. The animal uses its tongue to form a vacuum to suck clams into its mouth and to suck the flesh from the shell. A walrus has bristles on its upper lip. These bristles are sensitive to touch and probably help the walrus find food.*

JAMES: 'Right. Of course there will be false alarms, and your eyes are held up by the word "food" along the way, but better than being held up all along the way.

You must be alert to words related to the topic in which you're interested, like a detective looking for clues.'

DIGBY: 'It's quite strange really. If someone had asked me before how to locate specific information like this I would've been quite sure I was doing it correctly, but I see now that that's because I've never thought about it previously. I just took it for granted I knew how to do such a simple piece of research. Now I see how in every little aspect of reading, the chances are I'm not operating at my maximum efficiency.'

JAMES: 'As in so many matters, one needs to have one's inefficiencies pointed out.

Well, now we're ready to move up the scale of difficulty, because so far you've only skimmed in a narrow field, finding information which you're fairly sure will be there. That's only half the problem in skimming. The process becomes more difficult when you're not sure what you want, or if there's anything for you, but you know you'll recognize something of value when you come across it. It's like casting your eyes over panels of wallpaper, glossing over them till you instantly recognize something that appeals to you. Then you slow down and examine the one that appealed to you in more detail.'

DIGBY: 'And, no doubt, you have a method for tackling that aspect.'

JAMES: 'I have. The principles remain the same, only here you're asking yourself a different question. No

* From *The World Book Encyclopedia*, © 1988 World Book, Inc., Chicago.

longer are you asking what does the material say about so-and-so, and where do I find it; but rather, is there something here for me and what is it? You want the ideas, the main points which are of interest to you.'

DIGBY: 'Won't your "3T Method of Preview" do that? I've found it so useful in locating which articles of the dozens you've given me are worth going through.'

JAMES: 'Yes, but skimming is an extension of that, using the "3T" method plus other specific signs. But before we move onto that let's take a quick look at the structure which underlies all written material. As with all skills, I've said this before, it helps to know the underlying mechanics of what you're dealing with.

All written material is built up methodically, sentence by sentence, paragraph by paragraph, from beginning to end. No matter how badly written anything is, or muddled the thinking of the writer, he or she must build an article or book according to a basic pattern.

Beginning with its skeleton, its primary idea, all written material consists of sentences, paragraphs, and the whole unit. Cast your mind back a moment, to your school days. As you recall, sentences consist of actor-action-goal (subject-verb-object). Even the longest most convoluted sentence has, as its skeleton, the doer, what he's doing, to whom or what.

Consider the sentence in this newspaper article. "Mr John Smith, chairman of both the environment committee and the advisory committee, said yesterday that after the Eastbourne conference and the advisory's committee's recommendation there was a clear need for the parliamentary party to have as early an opportunity as possible to express its views to the Secretary of State."

The message is that Mr X felt there was a need for the parliamentary party to express its views to the Secretary of State. If you'd looked for that in the first instance your eyes would have skipped over the details of the committee and where it met, half the article in fact.

An efficient skimmer should be on the lookout for the basic substance of any sentence, in order to find at a glance the main point without bothering about its trimmings.

These sentences are then made up into paragraphs, each of which is a unit of thought containing a topic sentence, a main point which stands alone. The other sentences of the paragraph merely fill it out. You should learn to recognize this pivotal main idea as swiftly as possible.'

DIGBY: 'It's usually the first sentence, as you said.'

JAMES: 'Correct, about 80 per cent of the time, with about 10 per cent elsewhere in the paragraph, mostly the last sentence, and 10 per cent with no topic sentence. These usually just tell you more about the previous paragraphs.'

DIGBY: 'I must check that.'

JAMES: 'Do, but we'll skim an article presently and you can see if that bears out what I'm saying. But getting back to the structure of written material, the sentences and paragraphs build the whole article or book, which has a beginning, stating the case, the middle which develops it, and the ending, which draws the whole together.'

DIGBY: 'It reminds me of the film director's advice to his screen writers: "Tell 'em what you're gonna tell 'em, tell 'em, then tell 'em you've told 'em".'

JAMES: 'Sums it up perfectly. Understanding the structure of written material helps your approach to it. But there are other aids to your skimming.'

DIGBY: 'And these are?'

JAMES: 'Words. Key words, signals telling you where to go on fast ahead, when to slow down, and when to stop and take notice. They act like the signs on a motorway. If you take no notice of those along the way you'll miss your turn off, wasting time and energy. So with reading, you should notice the "directional" words which help you on your way.

Think of these three sets of words as traffic lights. *Green* words suggest you can go ahead, there is more of the same idea to follow. There are to be no changes, and as you already have the main idea you can fly on. Can you think of any words that do this?'

DIGBY: '*And*, I suppose.'

JAMES: 'Yes. *And* is the most common one, letting you know that more of the same is to follow, with the comma in most cases standing in place of the word "and". So when you see a string of them, get on with it, jump over them to the next point. For example: "the first settlers found plentiful food from the wild game in the forest – turkeys, deer, squirrels, rabbits . . . and so on." Any other words come to mind?'

DIGBY: '*Furthermore.*'

JAMES: 'Yes: "furthermore the settlers found nuts, berries, grapes and other wild fruits to eat." The word *also* is a perfect one to push you on. It literally means "all in the same manner". There are other words: *likewise, moreover.* Be aware of them as you skim along, you can safely speed up at these signals. You'll be surprised how they jump out at you next time you read and will get your eyes moving once you're attuned to them.

Now *yellow* words. They suggest a turn in the idea or thinking of a writer; tell you a change is about to occur and you must be ready for it. Take note of them and you'll be safe in getting the change of idea, same as if you take heed of the caution in a traffic light, you'll keep out of trouble. As we all know, crossing on a yellow light can be dangerous. Can you think of any words that suggest a turn in the idea or thinking of the writer? Another three letter very common word.'

DIGBY: '*But.*'

JAMES: 'Yes. "Oh, now comes that bitter word – but, which makes all nothing that was said before . . ." (Samuel Daniel). The word negates the preceding statements, implies a change. Take heed of it.

Other words and phrases which do the same are: *yet, nevertheless, otherwise, on the contrary, however.* They all prepare you for a change of idea and come either at the beginning of a sentence or between two clauses of a combined one. Watch out for them. Slow down and note the change. Again, now that I've told

you about them, you'll be on the lookout and they'll
jump out at you.'

DIGBY: 'Now the *red* words, I suppose.'

JAMES: 'Yes. The *red* words herald the summing up, the
conclusion, and you should pause. These words pull
the whole piece together. They include: *thus, so,
therefore, consequently, in conclusion.* They tend to
start a sentence and always hit out at you when
skimming. Mostly they're the topic sentences. If not,
let your eyes glide down to find a word that suggests
it's the topic sentence.'

DIGBY: 'It all sounds quite formidable, preparing for
skimming.'

JAMES: 'It all fits in to place. Armed with –

1 Your ability to recognize topic sentences,
2 Knowledge of the basic structure of paragraphs
   and patterns of writing construction, and
3 The refinements of recognizing and responding
   to signal words

you are ready to skim efficiently, using the "4T
Method of Skimming".

I've written down the procedure for you, an extension of the "3T Method of Preview". Here it is.'

[He hands Digby the following sheet.]

4T Method of Skimming – Top, Trail, Test and Tail

1 Read the first paragraph at your fastest speed of
   comprehension to discover the general topic, the
   introduction. Sometimes you may need to read
   the first two paragraphs, you'll judge.
   You've now 'topped' the piece.
2 Read the first sentence of each following paragraph till you come to the last paragraph.
   You've now 'trailed' the piece.
3 This is the addition to your 3T previewing. As
   well as reading the first sentence of each paragraph, let your eyes glide over the rest of it
   looking for important words, perhaps names,
   dates, accentuating the main idea. Always take

note of 'signal' words. Again, if the first sentence isn't the topic one, try the last, or gloss over it and you'll pick it up with the help of directional signal words. Remember, too, that if you discover the topic point from the first half of the sentence, there's no need to complete it.

You've now 'tested' the piece.

4 Read the last paragraph as the first.

You've now 'tailed' the piece.

'Before we look at an article, I want to point out your objectives in skimming. You're not attempting to read, understand or remember everything. If you find something you need, mark it and come back to it, or make a note of the page etc. If you can't get back to it, read through that section. That's the only occasion when you'll slow down.

Your skimming will help you locate and look over what you need. If a whole section is of no interest, skip it entirely, once you've established that its topic sentence is of no concern to you at this time. Don't feel guilty. Remember, as I've said over and over, the book is there to serve *your* purpose, not the writer's.

Let's try out the method on this article from *Business* magazine, January 1987, following step by step the "4T Method of Skimming". In order to give your reading an air of authenticity, we'll provide you with a specific purpose. You've been offered an interest in an electronic company that intends to manufacture facsimile machines. You're short of time, as usual. You come across this article while paging through *Business*. In your quick preview I presume you'll take account of the type of magazine, who it's aimed at, the date, and whether or not the information is recent – of vital significance in a case like this. If you don't know the author, you might know of Global Press, at least that it's a Washington-based news service, written in the US. You'll know if this would affect the information or not. By reading the bold print on each page, you'll already have a brief summary – Japan has leading role, slim chance for

Europe and States, no real predictions on the ultimate role of the fax. We haven't time now for you to skim the whole article, just do the first page and we'll discuss it.'

[Digby skims the article (see pages 112–117).]

JAMES: 'Right. I'll just number the first ten paragraphs so that we can run through them.

The first paragraph. I trust you didn't read it all. Almost immediately you can see the introduction is not the topic sentence, but merely cites an example – high telex charges of a company etc. The eye glides over the middle part, catching the phrase in inverted commas, that the fax saves X amount. Last sentence begins. *But*, a directional word suggesting a change is to occur – it's the topic one here – the machine is Japanese. Remember, the last sentence in a paragraph is the second most likely place to find the topic sentence.

Second paragraph. The scenario is repeated round the world. The eye, catching the figures down the paragraph, is reinforcing the statement – not necessary to read.

Paragraph three. No way but up. Figures catch your eye and, again, at this stage you don't need them. You want trends.

Paragraph four. Competition for share of market is fierce, especially among Japanese firms. The eye catches names of companies. Not necessary for you.

Paragraph five. Rest of world doesn't get a look in. The hyphens act like brackets, clues that they're extras padding out the main point. Again, the last sentence tells you the Japanese machines are superior.

Paragraph six tells you when the fax was first developed. Not vital for you to know at this stage, but if it is of course read it. The topic sentence has told you what to expect in it.

Paragraph seven. Reasons for phenomenal growth – again, telling you exactly what's in the paragraph. You may or may not be interested at this stage. If you wanted to know the reasons, your eye could glide down the paragraph till you saw the phrase "These include . . ."

Paragraph eight. More about the new machines.

Paragraph nine tells you something about the US companies producing facsimile machines – went into a slump – Japanese took over.

Paragraph ten tells you the leading US suppliers. Chances are you don't need details, won't even remember them, the list of names of companies that is.

Let's take one more paragraph. The next says Japanese machines captured the US market – reasons – you're bound to read those.

And so on through the pages. The point's been made. So far, of the eleven paragraphs we've skimmed, all except the first, which is unusual, have the topic sentence as the opening one, which makes very clear easy reading for you. Take advantage of the way it is written. Now we'll jump to the last paragraph or two.

The last section: "Last but not least . . . development of 'personal facsimile'. . ." The very last sentence – the fax's ultimate role – is mostly a repeat of the bold print on the left. You know it. Jump to the last sentence – Japanese forging ahead.

The whole article is about 3,500 words. To read it, even at 300 words per minute, fast for most readers, would take roughly twelve minutes, but it is possible to learn all the main points in about three and a half. Even if you double that time, it's still about half what it would take most people, and I doubt if they'd absorb more, or retain much beyond what could have been achieved by skimming the article. However, I've raced through it and not given you a chance to speak. Any comments?'

DIGBY: 'Only that it worked very well with this article and now I can see how in the past, I've read much more than I needed to.'

JAMES: 'It works well with most material. It's not that difficult when the first sentence isn't the topic one to find that out quickly.

Incidentally, if you looked back now at the piece

undreds of thousands of telex messages chattering their way around the globe were costing Insight International Tours of London a fortune. With offices in the US, Canada, Australia and New Zealand, and agents in other regions, the company had an annual telex bill that looked more like a telex number. When it decided to switch to fax, it saved "tens of thousands of pounds a year". But the real point is that the machine chosen, a Canon Fax 320 F, is Japanese.

It is a scenario that, with the phenomenal growth of facsimile transmission, is being repeated daily around the world. Sales of the machines – which transmit replicas of paper documents over telephone lines – are almost reminiscent of the personal computer boom five years ago. Already, more than one million have been installed in Japan, 550,000 in the US and some 70,000, about 25 per cent of the the European total, in the UK. But this time the Japanese have established a virtually unassailable lead.

There is no way for the industry to go but up. Manufacturers and analysts predict that total machines installed in the US will grow over the next five years to more than 1.2 million. Sales there are expected to top $600 million this year. Europe as a whole has an estimated 300,000 fax machines, and there were sales of 110,000 units last year – determining a growth rate is difficult because many machines replace earlier models. But in the UK, 12,500 machines were sold dur-

1980s, facsimile transmission was first developed during the 19th century. Alexander Bain, better known as an associate of the philosopher Jeremy Bentham, demonstrated the first facsimile machine in 1843. And a Londoner, F.C. Bakewell, invented a "copying telegraph" in 1850 that incorporated many of the techniques used in facsimile machines today. But it is only in the past five years that the technology has really taken off.

Reasons for the phenomenal growth are many and various. Prices have dropped by a full two-thirds since 1980 – good machines are now available for $2,500 – while transmission speeds, resolution, and reliability have improved dramatically. Businesses are discovering the advantages of fax over other forms of electronic communications. These include the ability to transmit graphics and pictures, lower transmission costs for the same volume of data, elimination of the need to retype documents, and the capability of most machines to double as low-volume copiers.

Some of the newest fax machines can be programmed to send documents without an operator present. And, because the machines are so easy to use, there is no need for trained operators. There are still, of course, far more telex than fax users, but already some fax directories – the UK Fax Book, for instance – have appeared. Inevitably, as the number of users grows, the usefulness of facsimile machines for inter-

company communications will increase.

Before the fax revolution, about 10 years ago, a handful of US companies – 3M, Xerox, Burroughs and Magnavox – dominated a market worth $100 million. But evolution of the fax market mirrored developments in other advanced technologies, such as that for photocopiers, where the Americans fell behind the Japanese. Pitney Bowes marketing director Meredith Fischer says: "The facsimile market went into a slump (in the 1970s), and by the time it got interesting again, the Japanese had it."

Now, in the US, Ricoh is thought to be the leading supplier, with 15 per cent of the market under its own name and another 15 per cent through a marketing agreement with AT&T. Matsushita is a close second, with something less than 15 per cent of the market through its subsidiary, Panafax, and another 15 per cent through a deal with Pitney Bowes. Canon is number three, with perhaps 10 per cent of the market, followed by NEC, Toshiba, Sharp, Fujitsu, Sanyo, Murata, Oki and Hitachi.

Japanese machines have captured the US market for several reasons, one of them domestic demand: there are twice as many facsimile machines in Japan as in the US. Another reason is that facsimile technology is especially suited to Japan, where handwritten documents are still a necessity (there is no completely satisfactory way of typing Kanji characters). A third reason is that facsimile technology is very similar to

The fact is the Japanese have a Sumo wrestler's hold on the multi-billion-dollar world facsimile transmission market. Europe and the US have only one chance, a slim one, to take a share of the spoils. Jeff Ubois on fax and the future.

FACING THE FAX

ing the third quarter of 1986, for a growth rate of 129 per cent.

Competition for a share of this burgeoning market, at least among the major Japanese manufacturers, is fierce. Precise figures are difficult to establish. But trade sources estimate that, worldwide, NEC holds the top spot, while Canon is number two and Matsushita's subsidiary, Panafax, is third. This, though, is strictly for branded machines: if machines sold under other companies' names are included, Panafax just might be number one.

What is far more easily determined is that the rest of the world – with the exception of France, whose Thomson CSF is the sole significant European manufacturer – does not get a look-in. All of the other European firms, such as Siemens, Flessey and Muirhead, market facsimile machines that are manufactured in Japan. And as one US speciality manufacturer candidly puts it: "The Americans didn't lose an opportunity to dominate the facsimile market. They never had a chance." The reason – "the Japanese machines were so superior".

For all the vigour of the competition and the vying to establish state-of-the-art machines in the copier technology: spin-offs from copier technology – scanning and printing, for example – have now been incorporated.

Even so, one US company, Telautograph, has been in the facsimile business for nearly a century. It was founded by Elisha Gray, an inventor of the telephone. (Gray and Alexander Bell filed their telephone patents on the same day, but Bell beat his rival to the patent office by a few hours; if Gray had arrived first there would never have been a Bell Telephone company.) The company's first facsimile product, the Telautograph, which transmitted over telegraph wires, was invented in 1895 by Gray and an Englishman, A.C. Cooper. Last year, the company sold 24,000 of its machines. Vice-president Frank May recalls that US manufacturers originally came out with slow, heavy-duty facsimiles for military, banking and other special applications. "The US had the market, but it was not a visible one," he says. "It was too small – whatever market there was, was too small to risk development costs on. The Americans didn't have any reason to develop the market. The Japanese have depended on facsimiles for years because of their handwriting system."

They had the need, so they produced facsimiles in huge numbers. They had been selling facsimiles in their country and they started shipping their surplus over here.

As is their way, the Japanese employed product standardisation, lower manufacturing costs, high quality, low prices, and effective marketing to their advantage. Standardisation, in particular, is an important element of Japan's success. Unlike the Japanese, US manufacturers were slow to adopt standards that were introduced about 10 years ago by a UN organisation called the Consultative Committee on Telephone and Telegraph (CCITT). These standards allow facsimiles, regardless of manufacturer, to communicate with one another. Before adopting the CCITT standards, US facsimiles were non-standard and incompatible. Each manufacturer, and sometimes each new model, used a different method of transmission. Diverse standards evolved because there was no central body to create industry-wide standards for facsimile transmission, and because US firms were trying to lock customers into their product line.

When facsimile machines were used exclusively for intra-company communications, incompatibility was no problem. Users bought their facsimile network from one vendor and were not expected to use the equipment to communicate outside the company. But in Japan, communication between companies was important, and so were industry standards. By adopting the

At this stage in the fax boom, few US companies are left in the manufacturing sector. Firms that offer facsimile machines buy them from Japan. Relations between the Japanese and the US firms that market their products are extremely complex.

six minutes to transmit a document, are now obsolete.

Standardisation has had the same effect on facsimiles that the emergence of the IBM PC has had on IBM-compatible personal computers – they have both become commodity items. Brand names and "bells and whistles" are not what sell the machines: price and availability does that. Yet years

mile purchased from Japan's NEC. Federal Express planned to install up to 50,000 of these facsimiles, dubbed "ZapMailers", in their customers' offices so that they could transmit documents to other customers who also had ZapMailers. This network of ZapMailers would replace Federal Express's system of couriers and airplanes that now provide overnight document and two-hour facsimile service.

The ZapMailer turned out Xerox-quality copies on plain white bond in seconds, rather than the somewhat murky image that standard facsimiles produce on thermostatic paper. But this quality was had at a price, which turned out to be fatal to the ZapMail concept. The ZapMailer itself was expensive ($200 a month minimum usage), especially compared with the new low-cost facsimiles on the market, and this price differential was not helped by a downturn in the yen-to-dollar exchange.

Perhaps the most lethal factor was that, because it was a Group IV machine, the ZapMailer was not compatible with standard Group III facsimiles. Federal Express hoped to make its ZapMail network the industry standard (which was the only way it could hope to sell a large number, since they were not compatible with other facsimiles). But there were already 500,000 facsimiles in the US and, by comparison, Federal Express placed no more than 7,000 ZapMailers. For most businessmen, ZapMail's increased quality did not justify the added ex-

After the need to standardise CCITT standards, Japanese manufacturers created a new market that encouraged communications between companies with different machines. Today, unlike the personal computer industry, which has yet to adopt a single communications standard, virtually all facsimile equipment manufacturers use CCITT standards. These have been developed (basically, the very latest standards stay slightly ahead of the technology) every three or four years. Group I, Group II, Group III and Group IV standards are simple for purchasers to understand and most of the higher group machines are downwardly compatible. This means most Group IIIs can send and receive using the Group II standard.

The primary differences between different facsimile groups are in transmission times and resolution. Group IV machines send high-resolution documents in as little as three seconds, but are not yet widely used for commercial purposes. Group III machines transmit documents digitally in less than one minute, often in less than 20 seconds, and at a relatively high resolution. Group II machines take about three minutes to transmit a document. The vast majority of machines produced will require Group III; Group I machines, which require

after the need to standardise was clear to most observers, one of the more successful US companies, Federal Express, recently lost more than $300 million trying to buck this trend by setting up a proprietary system called "ZapMail".

This most ambitious attempt to launch a state-of-the-art facsimile network was expected to bring the company's overnight delivery service into the electronic age, replacing its couriers and airplanes with Group IV facsimiles and satellites. But, in a dramatic turnaround, Federal Express announced that it was abandoning ZapMail in September, only weeks after it had announced plans for a major overhaul of the system. When it launched ZapMail in 1984, Federal Express said it planned to spend $1.2 billion on the system over 10 years. This investment would pay for a system that included some 50,000 facsimiles in customers' offices, computers, two satellites to be launched in 1988, and four satellite transmitting stations. Federal Express hoped to break even by early 1986 and anticipated annual revenue of $1.33 billion by 1988 and nearly triple that by 1995.

While the company might have been heading in the right direction to become a leading user of telecommunications technology (some analysts say it was premature for Federal Express to abandon ZapMail), industry observers say the way it set up its system was a classic case of mishandling newly emerging technology. The heart of the ZapMail system was a Group IV facsi-

pense. The quick service ZapMail provided had to compete with Federal Express's overnight courier service, which was already adequate for many businesses. And those companies that had to have faster, same-day service typically already had a Group III facsimile.

At this stage in the fax boom, few US companies are left in the manufacturing sector. Those firms that offer facsimile machines buy them from Japan. And relations between the Japanese manufacturers and the US companies that market their products are complex. Most of the agreements are straight OEM (original equipment manufacturer) arrangements, meaning that a US company will buy a Japanese machine and add its own label. For example, AT&T buys its machines from Ricoh under an OEM agreement. This works well for the Japanese manufacturers, which are then able to tap the brand loyalty of companies like AT&T. But in most cases, says Gary Winkler of Ricoh, it is the US firms that have sought out the Japanese.

In the past, joint ventures such as that between Burroughs and Fujitsu were more common. Under one of the first such ventures, Visual Sciences and Matsushita joined to form the Panafax company. Mat-

115

sushita later bought out Panafax and Visual Sciences was liquidated. Some observers say that Visual Sciences and Matsushita fell out over supplying facsimiles to Federal Express for ZapMail. Matsushita personnel associated with Panafax tried to bring the ZapMail order directly to Matsushita, thus bypassing Panafax and Visual Sciences. Now, US manufacturers are marginal, and have been forced into specialty areas, such as banking and law enforcement. Alden Electronics is making specialised machines, primarily large-format machines for transmitting satellite photos and weather maps. EG&G and Crossfield manufacture systems for the newspaper publishing industry, and Litton Datalog and Magmavox make systems for the military.

IBM threw in the towel last year when it purchased 3,000 Matsushita machines through Pitney Bowes for its own internal use. And with the advent of Japanese manufacturing in the US, perhaps the largest facsimile manufacturers in the country will be Japanese: NEC has a plant in Oregon, Ricoh has a plant in New Jersey and Canon is planning to open manufacturing facilities in Virginia.

rom the Japanese standpoint, developments in the US market follow those in their own domestic market – but about three

ful for applications related to personal computers, such as desktop publishing and graphics. Although scanner manufactuers such as Wang, Datacopy and Abaton will not be competing head-to-head with Japanese facsimile makers, they will cut into their market.

Not surprisingly, several large facsimile manufacturers, notably Canon and Ricoh, have also introduced scanners. It is predicted that this market will also go to the Japanese because scanning technology is so similar to facsimile technology. IBM's scanners, for example, are made in Japan and a Japanese company supplies Datacopy with its scanner hardware. Lawrence Gasman, president of Communications Industry Researchers in Washington and author of several studies on facsimile machines, believes virtual facsimile machines will outsell dedicated facsimile machines by more than two to one in the next 10 years. "The major threat to Group III is not Group IV, but facsimile scanners used with micros," Gasman says. "The combination is quite powerful. But, once again, I doubt if every micro user will want it and there will always be space for Group III dedicated terminals."

Already, there are several scanners and software packages for PCs that can capture and send a document the way a "real" facsimile machine would. Several companies, including IBM and AT&T, have scanners, and at least one of these scanners, sold by Pitney Bowes, doubles as an optical character reader. Scanners are comparable in price to a facsimile machine and there is a ready

Group III facsimile machine – with no paper printout required. The Gammafax board can receive incoming Group III transmissions. And Gammalink plans to upgrade its board so that it will run in "background" – while waiting to receive, or while accepting, an incoming message.

"Facsimile may be no longer a product line, but rather a technology that uses different means," says Jack Carlson of Alden Electronics. "Facsimile equipment conjures up rotating drums and flat-bed electrical systems, but now it will be based on a variety of different methods."

Clearly, technical developments will drive facsimile's future. Several key areas of innovation exist in addition to the virtual facsimile. One is the development of Group IV machines, which transmit documents over high-speed data lines in less than 10 seconds (sometimes less than five) at extremely high resolution. At present, Group IV is too expensive to be competitive with Group III; Group IV machines cost $12,000, compared with Group III machines that cost about $2,500, and they need special telephone lines costing several hundred dollars a month. Group IV will probably not gain a significant share for five years.

Related to Group IV technology is the development of dial-up, high-speed data networks, such as AT&T's Accunet service and ISDN (integrated services digital networks). The availability of cheap digital transmissions is necessary if Group IV is ever going to be used widely. "This technology is being driven by the availability of years later. Two areas in which this is particularly true are market size and growth rate. The US market in 1984, 1985 and 1986 was virtually a replay of Japan in 1981, 1982, and 1983. Another area of similarity is usage. Facsimile machines were used at first only by large companies—*Fortune 1000* firms accounted for nearly all of the market five years ago. Five years from now, they will account for less than half.

Two recent developments could help the US facsimile industry – or at least hurt the Japanese. One is the rise in the value of the yen. The price fall of machines from Japan has been stabilised at last, which means that sales might slow. "The yen is putting severe pressure on product markets," says Winkler of Ricoh. "There was the feeling that there would be price increases, but we have not seen much of that – severe price competition is taking place." Winkler adds that "gross profit margins were 40 to 50 per cent in 1985" and that, although prices have not gone up, Ricoh is still making a profit.

The second development – invention of the "virtual facsimile" machine – provides a chance for the Americans to get back in the market. The virtual facsimile is essentially a marriage of personal computer and scanning technology that achieves the same result as a facsimile machine, but more flexibly. Scanners convert any image on paper to electronic data, which can be electronically altered, stored or transmitted. This is use-

market for them among eight million users of personal computers in the US. One US firm, Gammalink, has developed a plug-in circuit board for IBM PCs and compatibles that eliminates the need for a facsimile machine. It sells for less than $1,000 and fits in a PC like any other board. Using the Gammafax software, users can take a standard text file and transmit it directly to a

> **Facsimile's ultimate role in telecommunications is all but impossible to forecast with any certainty. Predictions range from it replacing telex and courier services to disappearing as a distinct technology and being replaced by the PC and the new scanner.**

good phone lines as much as the demand for new phone lines is being driven by demand from the facsimile market," says Vincent Park of Panafax.

ast, but not least, is the development of the "personal facsimile". Canon, for example, is betting that simple, cheap facsimile machines, analogous to personal copiers, will grab a significant share of the market. The company introduced an integrated facsimile and telephone system last June designed to fill this niche. Named the Faxphone 10 and retailing for $2,495, the personal fax is seen as ideally suited to the needs of those who work at home.

Facsimile's ultimate role in telecommunications is all but impossible to forecast with any certainty. Predictions range from it moving to replace telex and courier services to it disappearing as a distinct technology and being replaced by the PC and the scanner. But while the West watches and waits, the Japanese are forging ahead to dominate yet another sector of the global economy.

Jeff Ubois is a writer for Global Press, a Washington-based news service.

This article is reproduced from *Business*, January 1987.

117

you previewed on depression in *Working Woman* magazine, and skim it, you may pick up a few extra points'.

DIGBY: 'I suppose the main problem is to get rid of the feeling of missing much of the information.'

JAMES: '*That's* the idea – to miss out information. By skimming you're finding not only the main contentions of the writer on a particular topic, but I would make two suggestions to overcome your fear of missing it all.

Firstly, skim articles you'd never think of looking at if not for this exercise, or look through a work-related book you'd never pick up in the first place. Whatever you learn from that will be more than you otherwise would have, and you'll be surprised at how much that is.

I remember one occasion when I was doing just that. I read an article on a new system of franchising businesses and by chance met a specialist in that field at a dinner party several days later. I was amazed, and amused, to see how I managed to chat to him, apparently quite knowledgeably on the subject, having only skimmed the article. That proved its value for me right then.

Secondly, I suggest that for a while you test your skimming by reading through any article you have skimmed. Do it with the "fax" article. You'll be able to judge how much of the main features you actually picked out from your skimming. This testing is important when you're skimming for vital information, such as material for this project you're working on. You should recheck till you're sure you have the hang of it.'

DIGBY: 'I'll try it all out.'

JAMES: 'Remember, you're not reading. You'll miss the richness of writing, the detail; but keep your purpose continually in mind and you won't feel too bad about it. You're not trying to absorb all the meaning, comprehending it all, you're simply taking note of what there is for you. You must be fully aware of that. How exactly you develop your active searching will depend on you.'

DIGBY: 'I suppose I can use this method successfully in reading newspapers?'

JAMES: 'We'll need to discuss that, and how to tackle skimming in the office. But we've had a long session today, leave it till next week.'

DIGBY: 'That's fine. I've enough to get on with. See you then and thanks.'

Summary

The four basic elements in skimming are: selecting, skipping, skimming and scanning.

Be on the alert for topic sentences.

Be on the alert for 'traffic light' words; the green that tell you to go on quickly, the yellow to caution you of a change to come, and the red which tell you to stop and look closely.

4T method of skimming

For an article or chapter:

1 Read first paragraph – top it.
2 Read first sentence of each following paragraph till the last one – trail it.
3 Let your eyes glide between each topic sentence picking up significant factors relating to it – test it.
4 Read the last paragraph – tail it.

Executive action

Try out the above method of skimming on several articles, both work-related and others of general interest, particularly on articles you would otherwise not have looked at. Afterwards consider what you have learned from your skimming. Test by reading in full and compare information gained.

9 Newspaper and workplace reading

DIGBY: 'Today, if I remember correctly, you're going to suggest a method of skimming newspapers.'

JAMES: 'Amongst other things, yes. But we'll start with those, for they represent one of the commonest daily habits of most literate adults. Over any week, the amount of time the average adult spends reading newspapers must vary enormously, but at a guess I'd imagine a couple of hours during the week, and the same on a Sunday. This could be reduced, leaving you time to read other papers, or other reading material.'

DIGBY: 'I've already found my improved reading skills get me through them in less time.'

JAMES: 'I'm sure, but in addition there's some specific help that's needed here. Reading newspapers should involve your most aggressive methods of attacking print. Always bear in mind that their primary function is to give you news, and yours to receive it.'

DIGBY: 'But you can't ignore the value of newspapers for the analysis, commentary and argument they offer on issues, surely, quite apart from the news?'

JAMES: 'Certainly not, but I'm talking here about their primary function of imparting news, and as this takes up so large a portion of the daily press, it's here you can capitalize on efficiency.

Be strict about how much you need from any news item. For instance, if you're reading about an accident or a legal battle, do you want just the main features, or have you a special interest or need to know the details – maybe friends or colleagues are involved? Don't waste your time reading with idle curiosity about incidents that you'll have forgotten almost as soon as you've put down the paper.

Also, you certainly need have no qualms in reading exclusively for meaning – there's no particular beauty in the language of a news report. With current affairs you read for information rather than for understanding. In other words, there's no excuse here for reading too slowly or "fondling" the words.

In addition to your general efficiency in reading, you should notice the layout and structure of newspapers.'

DIGBY: 'The narrow columns certainly help. I've learnt to read them downwards.'

JAMES: 'Yes, but I'm talking about layout in a wider sense. Most people are familiar with the layout of their favourite daily paper and of course they use this knowledge to skip over sections in which they're not interested, fashion, the arts, sports page, whatever. But, carrying this even further, there's so much information, why read incidental items which are not necessary to your knowledge of what's going on around you? They don't interest you particularly and generally serve no purpose. You'll be no wiser for having read them and you probably won't even remember them. So why bother?

As far as the structure of individual news items is concerned, you may know that a news article tends to be based on the inverted pyramid structure, that is, the first paragraph says it all. It usually answers the questions who, what, when, where. why and how. The summary is at the beginning. There's a twofold reasoning behind this. Firstly, it catches the attention of the reader immediately by telling you the main facts and, secondly, in the event of anything significant occurring in the world after the paper has been laid out, it's easier to chop off the bottoms of a whole lot of articles to create room for the additional important material, than it would be to rewrite or delete all the other articles.'

DIGBY: 'Really? I never knew that.'

JAMES: 'Well that's the general way it works. On the whole the important features of a news item are at the beginning, leaving you to do your own chopping off, so to speak.'

DIGBY: 'I'd never realized that. I shall look out for it this evening.'

JAMES: 'Another feature of newspaper structure that helps you to read them more easily is that news items, and I'm not talking here about editorials, special extraneous articles and so on, are written in simple sentences and are generally very explicit. There is no philosophizing in straightforward news reporting. Remember this and it will spur you on.

So, because of the simple structure and layout, you can run your eyes down the page and skim it in single fixations, anticipating, picking out topic phrases and sentences that tell you all you need to know.'

DIGBY: 'It'll be great to read through one paper and have enough time to take a look at a second.'

JAMES: 'A warning here which has nothing to do with the layout or structure of a newspaper, but to do with you: don't read what you already know. The purpose of reading news items is to make yourself aware of what's going on in the world. If you've already learned a particular item of news from the television, perhaps the most common way, there's no earthly point in going over it again. Often an article will repeat almost identically what you might have seen on TV the evening before, or heard on the radio. Similarly, reading the same report in an evening paper and then again in a morning one is unnecessary. The temptation is strong to do so, but ask yourself if it's so interesting that you need to go through it a second time.'

DIGBY: 'I am guilty there. I automatically read news I've heard on TV.'

JAMES: 'Try it on a single item of news you hear from the radio or TV and read it next morning. See if you learn anything worthwhile or remember anything more about it. Obviously there are exceptions and in some important items you do want additional material. But think about that first, don't read everything that's there. An old associate of mine told me how, since carrying out this resolution, she now manages to read her morning paper as well as reading material during her daily trip into London.

It seems to me that reading newspapers has become so common a daily habit – like cleaning your teeth at night that, just as the hygienist has to remind me every six months to brush my teeth correctly, so readers need to be reminded occasionally to put newspapers in perspective. One tends to read them so avidly.

Tell me, what do you remember having read in this morning's paper?'

DIGBY: 'The nurses' strike – picket?'

JAMES: 'What else?'

DIGBY: 'The continued fighting on the West Bank, um . . .'

JAMES: 'The items of news are certainly not flowing from you. What do you remember of yesterday's?'

DIGBY: 'I'll have to think that one out.'

JAMES: 'Last week?'

DIGBY: 'I give up.'

JAMES: 'In other words, not much is noteworthy, memorable, or of any lasting value to you.'

DIGBY: 'Well, not when you put it that way, no. But surely you aren't saying that reading newspapers is a waste of time?'

JAMES: 'Good heavens, no! Apart from informing us of the affairs of the world, any worthy newspaper is not only bringing our attention to what is happening in it, but is making us aware of dangers, infringements of our rights and liberties. It is usually newspapers that ferret out injustices and bring them to our notice. Hence in any totalitarian state it is often the Press who are blamed for causing the ills of the state which results in the banning of reporters.'

DIGBY: 'Like the kings of old who had messengers of bad news put to death.'

JAMES: 'Right. I'm really just suggesting that you keep the reading of newspapers in perspective. Take a visit to a reference library and look up any old newspaper, a single issue. You'll find that most of it is of very little value to you, quite meaningless in fact, because it's out of context, in another age. A newspaper is concerned with immediate happenings that lose all importance with the passage of time, apart from a few outstanding events. Only in accumulation do they tell you something of history.

However, newspapers do play an important role in our lives, and we need to read them and be highly critical of them. As in all non-fiction, you should be on the lookout for distortion, distinguishing fact from opinion. Newspapers are written to sell, and so they give the public what it wants – brightness and sensationalism – often sacrificing the truth in so doing.'

DIGBY: 'They certainly aren't there to cheer you up.'

JAMES: 'You're right. There's rarely anything in a single issue to brighten your day. We all know how newspapers are filled with bad news. People adore reading about conflict – they find good news boring.

It's a case of *caveat lector*, let the reader beware, particularly in his newspaper reading because that is, on average, the population's most regular form of reading, often the only one.

So you must put reading of newspapers into context in your life. Be aggressive in your perusal of them and always remember a newspaper is there to be read primarily for news. Of course I'm not ignoring the other articles, general ones, the type you read in magazines, but there's so much else to read, don't waste all your time on newspapers. It's not necessary to assimilate the entire contents of any one issue. Spend the extra time you gain either in reading something else, or in reflecting on the significance of what you've just read.'

DIGBY: 'I'll set myself a task – to read two newspapers, from different points of view, in the same time as I generally spend reading only one of them.'

JAMES: 'A good idea! And now we'll press on. I want to

say a few words about other perspectives in reading
– in your office.'

DIGBY: 'Oh good! I've become very aware of course of my
improved approach to reading. I'm certainly operating more efficiently, but I'm still not too good at
organizing my work reading; it's piling up in my
office.'

JAMES: 'Like every other aspect of your working life you
need to time-plan your reading at work. For a start,
make up your mind not to let it pile up in baskets,
files or drawers. Deal with each piece of reading
matter that lands on your desk, no matter how
briefly, as soon as it comes in – within reason of
course. Never just stack it away intending to get to
it at some later stage, you know that you never
will. This is an essential part of time-managing your
work reading.'

DIGBY: 'How on earth can I do that?'

JAMES: 'If you tackle everything, no matter how briefly,
as you receive it you'll be amazed how you can cope.
Some sort of selection or preview should be carried
out right away to eliminate part of it directly, and
then grade the others in order of importance.

Tell me all the forms of reading matter
submerging you in our office.'

DIGBY: 'Oh, letters, memoranda, reports, journals,
financial papers, advertising bumf, technical papers,
periodicals of all sorts.'

JAMES: 'And other extraneous reading matter that you
think will be of use to you some time.'

DIGBY: 'OK, so how do I deal with all that straight
away?'

JAMES: 'Let's look at the different sorts of material we
mentioned.

Basically there are two types of reading matter in
the office. In the first group are those, mostly by
non-professional writers, written or typed with a
particular message for a particular person or
persons. The second and larger group of printed
material is mostly by professional writers and aimed
at a wider and more general readership.

Those in the first group, the personalized written

or typed material, because they are by non-professional writers, tend to be less organized, more verbose and therefore often more difficult to read. But because they're for selected persons, you should first satisfy yourself that the letter or memo does concern you directly. Far too often memos and internal reports of some kind or other are circulated throughout a company and are read by staff who are not directly concerned. I can remember when I was a very young man I worked for a publishing company as a rep. The amount of bumf I received was unbelievable. In the beginning I used to read all of it until I realized I was wasting time and energy. Half the stuff was of no real concern to me. I was a rep for one section of books, but I was sent mail for all the other sections. I had to learn to select what I needed to function well in my particular job.

It is essential to do a brief preview to establish who exactly the memo or letter is aimed at. Be rigorous, it only takes a second or two. If it's not for you, throw it away instantly. The stacking of letters and memos for later perusal makes the whole process burdensome. You may already have the information through some other source – Mr X is becoming sales manager for instance, and you know it; the minutes of a meeting you attended and have no need to reread, or refer to again – discard it immediately. Have a large waste paper basket right alongside you. Trust your ability to nose out what's for you and shed what's not, without the slightest guilt.

In this way Marks and Spencer once made a revolutionary change in their office procedure and eliminated a vast amount of unnecessary paperwork. You should apply the same principle and eliminate all excess reading matter that reaches you. Keep your time and energy for more useful, informative reading – or some other important activity.'

DIGBY: 'What about all the letters that are specifically for me? How do I tackle those efficiently?'

JAMES: 'Bear in mind that they're not written by professional writers, and often contain more words than necessary. Be relentless and go straight to the heart of them.'

DIGBY: 'But there are so many different types – orders, acknowledgements, letters of information, complaints, recommendations, applications. How do I know where to find the main message?'

JAMES: 'I agree there are a great variety, but there tends to be a basic pattern to most business letters: the opening paragraph refers to a previous letter and date, the "hello, how are you" bit; the middle section contains the body of the letter with the main points; and the final paragraph invariably asks you to take some action. Go straight to the body of the letter for the main message. Hours are wasted in most offices reading the opening paragraphs. The letter head will tell you who it's from, so move directly to middle of the letter to establish if it's for you and what the main message is.

Dozens of letters are routine and the staff in a particular office can learn to recognize the general format of most of them and where to find the main part.'

DIGBY: 'Do advertising letters follow the same sort of pattern? I'm inundated with those.'

JAMES: 'They certainly start with the interest of the reader but gradually work through and end with the interest of the writer. Advertising copy is, of course, usually written by professionals, specialists in their field. I'll return to advertising material presently, but for the moment I'm still on the personal type of reading material you receive.'

DIGBY: 'Internal reports, I suppose.'

JAMES: 'Yes, and the most common fault with those is that the message tends to be hidden in extraneous verbiage. Often the writer indulges himself. Unlike magazines, where space is limited and not a word can be wasted, the writer of reports often has carte blanche to have his say – only his secretary might object to typing it all. But in your role as reader be ruthless, preview carefully and ask yourself if there is anything for you, and also whether or not you already know about it.

I think I've said enough on the matter for you to understand the idea and to know what to look out for. Now we'll move on to printed reading matter.

In some ways it's easier with professional writing because the writers are required to use their words more carefully, the advice of publishers always being "cut, cut, cut". Again, be ruthless and preview as soon as possible, eliminating at once what will be of no use to you.

In journals and books use the table of contents freely. It's your road map, a valuable part of the whole, telling you exactly what's in the volume. Mark precisely what you're going to look through, what you're going to preview.

Similarly with the index, which any reputable textbook has. Make a quick estimate of the range of topics covered, and the numbers of references under each topic. The complaint is frequently made that many postgraduate students show little awareness of the value of an index in a book.

Mark the articles you intend previewing at the very first opportunity you get when the journal lands on your desk. If you mark ahead what you intend going through, say two articles out of ten, psychologically the pile shrinks and becomes more approachable. When you pick it up next time you already know it's not so vast an amount.

Preview only those articles or chapters which you've marked as concerning you. In order to find the pulsebeat as soon as you can, you might like to turn straight to the last couple of pages, because this is where the author is most likely to sum up his thesis. I personally prefer, as in the "4T Method of Preview", to read the opening paragraph or paragraphs first. Look for the main points only. Put aside for later only that which you feel you must read more fully. Glancing at diagrams, graphs and charts often gives a dramatic insight into the text.

If you have masses to get through, do a short preview and leave those you've set aside for a second round preview.

One of the reasons you can race through your

initial resume is that, presumably, you're working within a field you're already familiar with. The more you know of the subject, the less of a new book or article on it do you need to read. Therefore, armed with your existing knowledge, you can forge ahead, omitting what you already know and taking only the essentials of what you don't. There's no time for idle curiosity in the office, unfortunately.'

DIGBY: 'Now I can see how great areas of print can be attacked, and eliminated when not required.'

JAMES: 'Exactly. Finally, a word on sales material, advertising bumf. These tend to follow a standard pattern or sequence.

1   Something is offered to attract the reader's attention.
2   The reader is told why an article or service will be of value to him or her.
3   The principal idea is stated.
4   Specific action is requested of the reader.

In other words – *Hey, You, Look, Do*.
    To be efficient, move rapidly to no. 3, and see what's on offer.'

DIGBY: 'Surely all advertising material doesn't follow the same format?'

JAMES: 'No, but I'm giving you some clues to help you search for the key messages. Discriminate, practise and adjust. Keep trying to improve your methods, your approach to all the different types of reading you come across in the office. You'll gain confidence as you go along. And you'll definitely save time and effort.'

DIGBY: 'You've given me plenty to think about.'

JAMES: 'More than think about, please – do it. Then you'll be able to reduce those piles of paper all over your office.

DIGBY: 'I'll try and make it as neat as yours. I often wondered how you managed to keep your office so paperfree. I used to think you just hid it all away.'

JAMES: 'You're welcome to look through my drawers.'

DIGBY: 'And find them empty. I hope to bring about a marked change in my office.'

JAMES: 'Good.'

DIGBY: 'Before I go I'd like to know how to approach digests like *Time* magazine and the *Readers Digest*. They're already summaries in a sense; long detailed information has been reduced to its essential elements.'

JAMES: 'I'm pleased you raised that. Yes, they present a specific challenge for, as you say, the solid core of information is extracted from the less substantial stuff. The greater the condensation, the more alert you must be to what is actually said. There is a slightly anomalous situation here. On the one hand you read a digest to save yourself going through reams of print and to get straight to the heart of the subject, which eases the job for you. On the other hand, because so much has been left out, you need to read between the lines, be on your guard, for you have to rely completely on the condenser's interpretation of the original. The writer of these condensed articles has to be a most skilful reader who can pick out the essentials, a difficult task. You need the skill to assess whether or not he's doing his job accurately. You have to rely implicitly on his judgement of what is important. So from that aspect, reading digests can become demanding.'

DIGBY: 'Isn't a lot lost in condensing written material?'

JAMES: 'It depends on the material. Most digest articles contain straightforward information that can condense well. Obviously a philosophical treatise would not. Digests serve a useful purpose in this busy world of ours, but must be viewed for the limited vision they give us on any topic.'

DIGBY: 'One thing which I find strange about digests is that, though they give you the main points on a topic, I have trouble remembering afterwards what I've read. Shouldn't it stay with me longer, because it's only stating the main message and there's less to remember?'

JAMES: 'That's an interesting point, but we'll talk about memory next week. For the moment I suggest that the reason you recall less from reading digests or summaries is that you yourself are not actively involved in taking out the main message. In reading, you're seeking, selecting, deciding what's important for yourself. With digests you're sitting back and passively accepting what's given to you on a plate, as it were. Think of the word "digests" – the material is already partially digested for you, the reward is not the same. Imagine eating all your food liquidized – at times it's welcome, but hardly when you're spending an evening out at dinner.

So don't confuse reading a digest with your own skipping and skimming and eliminating detail. Your doing it makes the big difference.

Let's take an analogy from life. You visit an art exhibition and find later that you've missed one of the paintings which was highly praised by a friend. You may well feel irritated, but you made your own choice and didn't have time to see all in your lunch hour. But suppose someone were to insist you only see what he or she considers worth viewing, you'd have far more cause to be disgruntled.

Again let me remind you that you should feel satisfied and content to recall those paintings you did see. Consider the value of what you achieved, rather than worry about what you did not – a piece of general advice which applies equally to reading.

Well, that's enough for today. Take a new look at newspapers, and keep your work-related reading well under control.'

DIGBY: 'Thanks, and see you next week.'

Summary

When reading newspapers:

> Read narrow columns downwards.
> Take advantage of the inverted pyramid structure of news articles.
> Don't read what you already know via some other medium.
> Keep your newspaper reading in perspective. Leave time for other reading.

In the office:

> Don't allow incoming reading matter to pile up. Do an initial preview and discard what's not for you.
>
> Most written or typed correspondence is non-professionally written. Search out only those parts relevant to you.
>
> The general structure of advertising material is:
>> *Hey*
>> *You*
>> *Look* – main message
>> *Do*.
>
> Be ruthless in dealing with reading matter in the office.

Executive action

Try tomorrow to look through two newspapers in the same time you normally read one.

Deal with your incoming office reading immediately from now on. With all incoming letters head straight for the main body – the central part.

In reading advertising matter, go straight to the *Look* part of the *Hey, You, Look, Do* structure.

10   Improving your memory

JAMES: 'Skimming your way through the XX material?'

DIGBY: 'I am – I'm surging ahead. What's more, I remember more of the information I take out from my skimming. As you said, it must be because I'm searching for the main points myself.'

JAMES: 'Yes, you're concentrating with a purpose.'

DIGBY: 'I still have a problem remembering everything I read, especially when I need to fix a whole lot of detailed facts into my head. I can't seem to learn things easily.'

JAMES: 'What exactly do you mean by learning?'

DIGBY: 'Committing to memory – being able to recall at a later stage what I've read. I have a poor memory.'

JAMES: 'There's no such thing as a good or bad memory. If you think about it you'll agree that you have no difficulty in remembering some things well, while others you can't at all. I've noticed, for example, that you can easily recall old football scores going way back.'

DIGBY: 'You mean because I'm interested in football? But I am in my work.'

JAMES: 'Let's say that remembering depends on various factors. Napoleon was said to have a dreadful memory, yet he managed to plan army manoeuvres in his head. When you think of it, even the most uneducated leaders many centuries ago managed to plan invasions down to every last detail without being able to write them down. So the whole process of remembering is obviously more complicated than the simple concept of a good or bad memory.

Everyone needs to retain information and be able to recall it later. In that sense everyone, though they may not be studying in the formal sense, needs to know how to study efficiently. You have to store information and recall it in your work in order to make a business pitch, to prepare and deliver a speech. And apart from work, I'm sure you need to collect and recall information for a host of other things, a hobby perhaps.

Of course in this modern world, to study or learn without the use of books, the written word in some form or other, is virtually unthinkable.'

DIGBY: 'And you're going to tell me now that there's a way to approach the printed word with a view to studying – remembering – from it.'

JAMES: 'Of course. What's extraordinary is that so few people approach the subject of studying books with any systematic plan in mind. Very few people ever learn to learn. And, as with all the other aspects of your reading, you need the correct approach in order to get the best results and save time and energy.

So let's return to memory as part of the learning process. On this we can then base our method of using books within this context. Memory, that is the ability to store information, retain it and retrieve it at a later stage involves several elements: motivation, registration, consolidation and confirmation. We'll deal with motivation first.

The more motivated you are to retain some information, the more likely you are to succeed, as with everything. Your general motivation in undertaking a particular project we can take for granted. I'm suggesting something more specific here.

You must identify a specific reason or purpose for every section or aspect of information you need to retain. This provides a psychological impetus for each section you approach, helps you focus attention on it and spurs you on. It helps you establish in your mind just why you need to learn, to retain that particular piece of information.

This identifying of reason inspires concentration and overcomes the fault of charging ahead without any goal or motivation. You'll then be fully active and retain it more successfully.'

DIGBY: 'Motivation is important in achieving anything.'

JAMES: 'The second factor is registration. Any piece of information you hope to recall at a later stage must be firmly registered or planted in your brain in the first place; in the same way that a better print on a fabric lasts longer than a poor one, an indelible pencil mark remains longer than an ordinary lead one. If an idea, a fact, is not fixed firmly in your mind, it can never be held there and recalled later. As William James maintained: "All improvement in memory consists in the improvement in one's habitual methods of recording facts." '

DIGBY: 'Easier said than done. The question is, how do you do it?'

JAMES: 'Through understanding. The material must be meaningful to you or you can't retain it for long. Think of a list of nonsense syllables or a passage in a foreign language. The only way you can learn them with comparative ease and keep them in your mind is by making them meaningful to yourself, by relating them to something that's meaningful, and making that image in your mind as vivid as possible.'

DIGBY: 'But that's only for single simple facts surely?'

JAMES: 'No, but that's always the best place to start. Let's take an easy example – the spelling of words. Ever had trouble remembering which is the verb and which the noun in practise and practice?'

DIGBY: 'Funnily enough, I still have to stop and think about it.'

JAMES: 'Well I solved that one many years ago by creating a meaning for the two letters s and c. I think of the letter "s" in practise, the verb, as being active (because there's more movement in the letter "s" than the letter "c"), so it's doing something, it's the verb. In practice, on the other hand, the "c" has less movement (it's a simpler letter), and therefore it's the noun. I can never go wrong now.

Here's another example. I always used to have trouble remembering whether the word occasion had two s's or two c's, till I formed a clear picture in my mind, though an absurd one, of the two cc's as in occult. I visualize the two cc's as two eyes staring into the unknown, creating an occasion. It'll sound ridiculous to you, and you can see no possible connection between the two words, but it has meaning for me, and it's indelibly set there. I should mention that whatever meaning you create for registering a fact, it must be of your own creation. You can't use other people's. It's a personal matter.'

DIGBY: 'Stationary and stationery. I have to think about them sometimes.'

JAMES: 'Think of envelopes as stationery, the "e" will tell you how to spell stationery.'

DIGBY: 'Thanks, I doubt if I'll ever get that muddled again.'

JAMES: 'Do you remember the difference between stalactites and stalagmites? I think of someone being "tight" – drunk, and hanging upside down. My daughter thinks of a pair of tights hanging down on a washing line. Neither of us can ever forget that stalactites are icicles that hang down from the roof of a cave and, obversely, that stalagmites come up from the ground. Come to think of it, you could think of mites as being little ones, close to the ground, coming off it. The scope is enormous.

At school we had to remember dozens of American cities and their industries. Taking but one example, I can never think of Toronto without picturing a waterfall (Niagara) with furniture and paper pouring over it. If Toronto has by now changed its main industries, I apologize.'

DIGBY: 'Mind you, I use a form of association for remembering telephone numbers.'

JAMES: 'Right. It's the same principle and can be developed. I suppose you create a story for each telephone number?'

DIGBY: 'Yes, I relate it to a date if I can. One friend's number is 1497 – the introductory code is easy to recall when you know the area – and I remember it as five years after Christopher Columbus discovered America.'

JAMES: 'All memory systems, mnemonics, are based on this law of association – forming meaningful patterns for you. The pattern facilitates recording in the brain. One of the reasons why oriental scriptures were mainly written in rhyme was to make it easier to remember because of the patterning. Anyone who ever had to learn poetry by heart must have found it easier to learn poems with rhyming lines because they create a pattern.

When you're tackling a poem or a speech you wish to commit to memory, do it in meaningful units, not line by line, or sentence by sentence. I once heard an actress on the radio say how she could only learn her parts in context, by acting them, thinking of their meaning, and then gradually the actual words came to her.

Paderewski was said to have studied other people's music by analysing it before he attempted to play it, noting its moods, themes etc., and only that way could he learn it by heart.'

DIGBY: 'Being active that way I suppose always helps it to register?'

JAMES: 'Yes. Laziness lets us take the easy way out in memorizing by rote, passively, without any creative effort. In the end it leads to frequent disappointment in retaining information and thus no short cut at all.

Now I'd like to give you a simple yet effective scheme for remembering items, whether a list of individual items, topic words for essays, speeches, information of any sort. We'll only do it for ten items, how you develop the system is up to you. I once read of someone who could recall up to one hundred items using this simple system.

Write down the numbers one to ten on a sheet of paper.'

[Digby does so.]

'Now find a common word that rhymes with each,

the first that comes to mind. I'll set you off. One –
bun; two – shoe; three?'

DIGBY: 'Tree.'

JAMES: 'Four?'

DIGBY: 'Door.'

JAMES: 'Five?'

DIGBY: 'Hive.'

JAMES: 'Six?'

DIGBY: 'Sticks.'

JAMES: 'Seven?'

DIGBY: 'Heaven.'

JAMES: 'Eight?'

DIGBY: 'Plate.'

JAMES: 'Nine?'

DIGBY: 'Swine.'

JAMES: 'Ten?'

DIGBY: 'Hen.'

JAMES: 'Most people come up with very similar lists.
Once yours is in your head you can always recall it.
Now, imagine the following is a list of things you
have to do the next day at work. It's the middle of
the night, you haven't a pen by your bed and you
don't want to switch on the light. Let's create a
list. Write down each activity next to your list of
numbers. I'll start you off. One – Buy mother-in-
law's birthday present. Two – you give one.'

DIGBY: 'Phone my solicitor.'

JAMES: 'Three – answer that letter of complaint you
received from the irate client.'

DIGBY: 'Four – order a new cheque book.'

JAMES: 'Five – send flowers to the sick secretary.'

DIGBY: 'Six – buy the management book that's just come
out.'

JAMES: 'Seven – find out time of PM's speech on the
radio.'

DIGBY: 'Eight – book flight to New York.'

JAMES: 'Nine – contact picture library.'

DIGBY: 'Ten – send in my monthly return.'

JAMES: 'Well that's our ten things, now show me the list.'

1 – bun – mother-in-law's present
2 – shoe – phone solicitor

3 – tree – answer letter of complaint
4 – door – order new cheque book
5 – hive – flowers to secretary
6 – sticks – buy new management book
7 – heaven – PM's speech on radio
8 – plate – flight to New York
9 – swine – contact picture library
10 – hen – send in monthly return.

JAMES: 'Now go through each and quickly make an association in your mind for each of the items with the numbered word. For example number one – mother-in-law's present. Perhaps picture handing her a packet of delicious iced decorated buns. Visualize them fully. On the other hand, if you can't stand your mother-in-law, you might like to picture throwing the iced buns at her. Actually, the more bizarre the mind picture, the more you're likely to remember it. A list of ten mind pictures shouldn't take more than a minute or so once you're used to the method.'

[Digby spends a minute or two creating visual pictures for the items on the list.]

JAMES: Turn over your list and tell me what item number five was.'

DIGBY: 'Flowers to the secretary.'

JAMES: 'What mind picture did you form for it?'

DIGBY: 'I pictured a beehive with flowers growing out of it and trailing down, bees sucking at them.'

JAMES: 'What was number eight on your list?'

DIGBY: 'Book flight to New York. I pictured myself getting there on a flying plate.'

JAMES: 'Write the whole list out now.'

DIGBY: 'The only one I can't remember is number three.'

JAMES: 'It was – answer letter of complaint.'

DIGBY: 'Ah, yes! I thought of the letters hanging from the branches of a tree.'

JAMES: 'Your association was too ordinary, too uncreative for your mind to record it. If you'd thought of something like a proclamation of olden days nailed to a tree, I'm sure you'd have remembered it.

I believe you'd have no trouble recalling that list for as long as you needed to. Once you had no more use for it, it would pass from your mind. If I say now, with it fixed in your mind, rethinking number three, retain it till next week – you will. See if you can. Try it on lists of your own and see how you go.

I find it invaluable for forming topic points in my head when I'm making a presentation. I hate using notes.'

DIGBY: 'I'm sure it'll come in handy. I shall certainly try it.'

JAMES: 'Time we went ahead now with the third element in the process of remembering, consolidation. Once you've registered the facts you wish to recall later in your brain, you need to consolidate, to keep them there.

It has been shown that the fastest loss of retention is immediately after learning. This is known as Ebbinghaus's "curve of learning". The theory is the opposite of rolling down a hill where you gather momentum and increase your speed as you go along – a snowballing effect. In other words, the largest loss is the initial one, and it then becomes more gradual.'

DIGBY: 'So directly after learning I must consolidate.'

JAMES: 'That's it exactly – almost immediately after the initial learning, to stop the quick loss of retention, to make the information set in your brain. Studies have revealed that 80 per cent of what has been studied is forgotten within two weeks, whereas when the work is reviewed immediately after the reading and registering the amount forgotten is only 20 per cent. After this initial review, subsequent ones at various intervals are necessary; each of which stabilizes your learning at a higher level.'

DIGBY: 'How do I set about consolidating? How do I review what I've just learnt?'

JAMES: 'At this stage we're not discussing study techniques, remember, but the elements that underlie them and on which you can base your study methods.'

DIGBY: 'Yes, of course. I forgot.'

JAMES: 'The fourth and final element involved in learning is confirmation.

You've set your purpose well for learning something, motivated yourself, registered it so that it's firmly fixed in your mind, and then you've gone over it soon after the initial learning and periodically after that. Now you should have no problem in recalling it at a later stage to confirm you have it in your mind. It's not fair to yourself to claim a bad memory at this stage unless you've made sure you've followed all the other stages. Take the example of remembering people's names and now think about it. Do you actively register the names of the people you meet in the first place? I'm sure you'd have no trouble in remembering the name of someone you meet in whom you're interested and wish to know better, and if you deliberately form an association of one person's name with something or someone in your past experience, you'll retain it.'

DIGBY: 'That's true.'

JAMES: 'So, to summarize, there are four elements involved in the process of remembering: motivation, registration, consolidation and confirmation.

MRCC, or MRC2 – find your own pattern for remembering the four elements, and you'll never forget them. But I'll leave it to you to make your own.'

DIGBY: 'I quite fancy MR Co Co, from the four letters.'

JAMES: 'Very good, now you have the hang of it. Next week we'll look at how to use these elements in creating a pattern or method of study. That is, how to record, remember and recall at a later stage. So for the moment just keep on with all the reading skills we've covered so far, and in addition, try out the 1 – 10 simple form of mnemonics. See you next Wednesday.'

DIGBY: 'Thanks, and cheerio.'

Summary

Memory involves four factors:

> Motivation. Find a reason for studying each section you approach.
> Registration. Fix information in your head by some form of association.
> Consolidation. Go over the material immediately after first learning.
> Confirmation. Go over material at various intervals.

Executive action

Try out the 1 – 10 scheme of association for remembering lists at home and at work.

11   Using books for study

JAMES: 'Today we're going to work on "MR Co Co" – your invention, and see how he, or rather the four elements he stands for – motivation, registration, consolidation and confirmation – can be incorporated into a system that will help you to extract information, record and retain it and finally recall it from all written or printed matter.

But before we do that, I want you to write out the list of things you had to remember.'

[Digby does so.]

JAMES: 'I see you remembered number three this time.'
DIGBY: 'Yes. I pictured a complaint of dogs fouling the tree in the park we use and a complaint hung on it.'
JAMES: 'Good, so you've got the hang of it. Now let's practise using the four elements of learning.

I don't intend to give you a set formula as such. There are thousands of these put forward in dozens of books, but I don't believe there is one single technique or way to study from books. What I do feel, as I'm sure has come across in these sessions, is that some specific procedure must be followed in all the aspects of reading. I'll suggest an outline amalgamating different ideas, adding specific tips. How you adapt or use this method to suit your own needs and inclination, personality even, is up to you. Take from it what you feel will be useful.. There should be something in what I suggest to help you record, retain and recall any information you extract from books.'

DIGBY: 'I could do with some help in that field.'

JAMES: 'I'm sure most people can. Unfortunately right at the start in schools, teachers tend to tell their pupils to learn some section in a book, rather than set specific tasks for homework in their reading. They are seldom directed as to what type of information is required, the general implication being that all the text must be read and known. Little is asked or expected of them in the way of reorganization of the information in the set piece, and this is unrealistic.

Even after school, studies, such as one in Sheffield university, found that the students generally were uninstructed in the all round use of books. They read slowly, couldn't select essential elements from the text or make usable notes from it. This made it difficult for them to collate and organize the information they did take down.

So the first step in preparing to extract information from books is to decide how much you can get through in one session. If you have two hours, say, in which to work, set yourself a reasonable chunk of reading matter to deal with. There's nothing more demoralizing than to face reams and reams of print with no end in sight. Setting yourself a fair, but not unreasonable, amount of material gives you an incentive to get on with it.'

DIGBY: 'Would you say that it's better to set yourself too little?'

JAMES: 'Yes, but don't overdo it of course. If you finish before time, good for you. Use the extra time to suit yourself and it'll inspire you to forge ahead at the next session. You'll soon learn to judge how much material to allow yourself for a set period of time.

Having chosen the section you're to deal with, the next step, which will come as no surprise at this stage, is to establish your purpose in setting out to register and retain that particular information.

Frame in words your reasons for requiring that information. There's your general purpose, of course, such as needing material for a presentation, to compile a manual for your sales staff. But you should narrow this down for each section. Why do you need it? What do you expect to gain from it to help you? Write this down, then there's no excuse for woolly thinking. By explicitly establishing this, you'll be motivated to go ahead.'

DIGBY: 'And I presume the same applies here as with all reading? I need to preview to help establish my purpose and know what to expect from a piece.'

JAMES: 'Yes. By establishing what you can expect, you can be helped to adjust to the piece. The bird's eye view gives you an idea of what you're "in for".'

DIGBY: 'If I was a student who had to learn a piece whether I wanted to or not – perhaps I felt it was a waste of time, like my kids on occasion at school – how then could I motivate myself to learn it efficiently?'

JAMES: 'If you try hard enough, you can find at least one reason why it's worth your while to learn something. Create a reason if necessary. Imagine you need it for such and such and that in itself can drive you on. Be active, you'll find you'll enjoy it more too. If all else fails, motivate yourself by bribery. Offer yourself a reward at the end of having studied something – half an hour lazing in the sun perhaps – and stick rigidly to it.'

DIGBY: 'A Mars Bar would get me going.'

JAMES: 'Right. So, after previewing the piece you've set aside for that session, the next active step is – hold it – you tell me. What was the essence of your active reading as we discussed?'

DIGBY: 'Asking questions.'

JAMES: 'Correct – and that's what you must do next at this stage of your studying. To help you find the answers, the information you need to extract and retain, you must first deliberately ask the questions that will produce the information you need.'

DIGBY: 'Specific questions again?'

JAMES: 'Questions based on what the piece is to tell you. That is, turn the subheadings of each mini-section into a question. If there are none, turn the topic sentence obtained by your preview, probably the first sentence, into a question.

I feel very strongly about carrying out this step, though in certain circumstances I do deviate in favour of another which I'll tell you about in good time. In the meantime I'd like to illustrate the value of asking questions from my personal experience.

Many years ago in my teaching days I was taking a geography lesson with a group of rather rowdy twelve-year-olds. I wanted to show them a film on the subject of city pollution. I made the mistake of showing the film to the first group without setting questions beforehand. The boys and girls passed a happy thirty minutes, paying very little attention to the film and did rather poorly on a questionnaire on the film's contents which was given to them afterwards.

For the subsequent groups, I presented them with a questionnaire which was to be read before the film was shown and not answered during the showing. I kept strict watch over that. I asked questions such as: How many different types of pollution occur in cities? What is the best way to handle waste disposal, motor exhaust fumes and so on? These groups were quieter during the showing of the film and concentrated more. They focused on what they were required to "do with" the material in front of them. They had been shown in advance what the main features were to be. Needless to say, they did much better afterwards in answering the questions. All the groups handled this way did better than the first group who were given no preview of what was to come, were set no questions, not geared to answer or look specifically for anything.

In my opinion the same applies to reading. But of course, such findings are borne out by other investigations of a similar nature.

Actively looking for answers is always more effective than waiting for some facts to "sink in" of their own accord while you read on passively. The chances are that they'll "float by" rather than "sink in". But don't rely on this evidence, test it out yourself with your own reading.'

DIGBY: 'The principle makes sense. Perhaps in schools they should train children to read the questions before reading a comprehension passage.'

JAMES: 'On the whole that is strongly discouraged, but it might well prove profitable. Of course no one would suggest that with long complicated comprehension pieces they could recall all the questions, but I do think they'd set the tone and make the pupil more aware. Perhaps some teachers should try the method.

In summary then, let's say that reading with specific questions in mind works because:

1 It provides a specific purpose, that is you're looking for a specific answer.
2 It focuses attention on the subject matter.
3 It keeps the mind from wandering.
4 It's all aimed at speeding up and consolidating the process of learning.'

DIGBY: 'Is there a format for writing down the questions?'

JAMES: 'The simplest and clearest is to draw a line down the centre of a sheet of paper and write each question on the lefthand side, leaving a reasonable space between each, determined by the nature of the material, its length, its depth of information and so on. The answers, as you come across them, can then be set out in the righthand column opposite the corresponding question.

Having drawn up your list of questions, you have to set about finding the answers. Your aim is to find and understand the answers, not to remember them at this stage. If you do, of course, that's fine.

Now, read the piece. Note, only at this stage after previewing, preparing your questions, do you begin to actually read through. As you come across the answers to the questions you've set yourself, jot down the key words and phrases in the righthand column. Don't copy reams of stuff from the book. This is sheer laziness and delays your registering.

I'm sure you've experienced how easy it is to take notes, underline and so on, without concentrating at all on the contents, the real information itself. Rather note the pages to which you might need to refer again later for details.

Never study without a pen or pencil in your hand. This is not only to write the answers alongside the questions on your sheet of paper but also the book itself if you possibly can, making comments as you go along.'

DIGBY: 'Write in books? That sounds quite heretical to someone whose first lesson on using books was not to write in them.'

JAMES: 'I'm not suggesting you write in your first editions, or in your glossy books where part of their value lies in the paper and print itself, or in anyone else's book, but the only value in most mass-produced books today lies in their contents and, more especially, the value of the contents to you, the reader. With the advent of paperbacks the chances are that whatever you're studying from can be used, written in, as part of the use process. They are not in themselves objects of beauty and value and should not be protected as such.

In order to make a book part of you, in the sense that a suit or dress hanging in the wardrobe only becomes part of you when you wear it, there should be some visible sign of your "conversation" with the writer of whatever you're reading in depth, taking instruction or information from.

I am far more impressed by someone's bookshelves when the books in them look well thumbed and written in, therefore used and loved, than by rows and rows of pristine volumes obviously untouched, no matter how expensive or rare they may be. It's rather like the contrast between a room that's been designed by an interior decorator with everything perfectly matched and toned but unused and lifeless, and a well worn room full of loved articles and pictures selected by the owner, full of atmosphere and personality.'

DIGBY: 'Or like a score of music to a conductor. I've seen

some which are positively criss-crossed with personal notations.'

JAMES: 'That's a good analogy. A book is the vehicle by which the reader gains his information, and the very act of making notes, commenting "verbally" on the material you read, keeps you mentally active and alert.'

DIGBY: 'Point taken. And are there any specific places in a book I should write in?'

JAMES: 'There are lots of convenient places – in the front and back of the book for a start there are usually blank pages, also the top and bottom of each page and of course, the margins.'

DIGBY: 'What about marking the text itself?'

JAMES: 'Use your imagination here. Create your own signs if you wish. Otherwise resort to the usual ones of vertical lines, asterisks, question marks, crosses, key words and phrases, arrows. I specifically don't recommend underlining because it tends to get out of hand and become indiscriminate. Rather encircle phrases, it's difficult to make those too large. Incidentally, highlite pens are useful for colouring the area while the words remain clear.'

DIGBY: 'But, getting back to my XX Project, most of the material I'm working from, all of it really, isn't mine. It seems to me that this can apply only to a student with his own books.'

JAMES: 'Now then Digby, think about it. There's a photo-copying machine at your disposal, as you know, for the articles I've given you. A few pages of an article compared to the wastage in that room is minimal. In other cases, it's for you to judge. Magazines can well be written in if you have permission from whoever's in charge of them. Maybe your comments in an isolated article in a not-worth-keeping maga-zine would enhance it for the next reader. I've picked up books in secondhand book shops and formed posi-tive attachments to those with sensible comments inside them. For example, I quite value my copy of Bertrand Russell's *Power* picked up for a few bob, which is full of a former owner's detailed comments. I can only think it came to be sold after his or her death. I couldn't imagine someone parting with a book in which so many of his own thoughts were written down.'

DIGBY: 'What about journal articles which are very long?'

JAMES: 'In the last resort you can make notes on a pad alongside the book if you really can't photocopy it or write in it. Don't write long sentences because it's only too easy to take them down passively while your mind strays elsewhere. Too much copying merely postpones learning, and leaves the information in the book or on your written pad. Only when you can recall in your own words are you learning.'

DIGBY: 'I'm interested to see how this all works in practice.'

JAMES: 'Try it out on one short section in any business textbook or article.'

DIGBY: 'Yes, I will.'

JAMES: 'Once all the information you want to understand is there for you, what's the next stage?'

DIGBY: 'To get it into your head, to register it.'

JAMES: 'Right, and you need to manipulate the information so that it's clearly and visibly set in your mind. Visual impressions are usually more lasting than verbal ones. For most people viewing a starving child in Africa has more impact than reading even the most vivid description.

Based on this premise, any transcribing of verbal information into visual patterns will help you to record it in your brain. Visual recall patterns show well-organized information with clear relationships'.

DIGBY: 'Do you mean like a family tree?'

JAMES: 'That illustrates the point admirably. At a glance you can see the relationship of any one king in British history for example, to any other, whereas reading through a written history of British royalty would be cumbersone, time consuming, and far more muddling.'

DIGBY: 'But can all information be recorded visually, as you put it?'

JAMES: 'In some form of planned visual pattern, yes I'd

say. The devices you use to achieve this can be as varied as you choose, and as highly individual. In fact the more creativity you use in planning your visual patterns, the more likely they are to stay in your head.

Also, the active process of forming, planning and designing visual patterns involves more senses and therefore, since each complements the other, helps cement the facts in your brain.

If you've ever drawn up any charts, graphs or diagrams for any purpose, I'm sure you've recalled them more clearly and for longer periods than a page of rambling print on the same subject.'

DIGBY: 'Yes indeed.'

JAMES: 'You must, of course, create your own individual pattern. The form of this pattern is determined either by the nature of the material you're dealing with, or by your own personality or behaviour. A more analytically minded person, for instance, tends to prefer the formal or abstract diagrams. This sort of thing.'

[James sketches a few diagrams for Digby (see p. 152).]

'As you can see, the variations are endless.

But the more expressive types of personality don't always have the patience for these, and use a more random or pictorial style.'

DIGBY: 'Can you illustrate these for me?'

JAMES: 'Yes, I'll use a concrete example. I noticed recently a representative for a publishing company painstakingly taking copious notes on all the selling points for each new book, resulting in sheets of paper each indistinguishable from the rest. I also know of a science director of a large educational publishing company who presents his new books at conferences as visual patterns.

I have a couple of photocopied sheets which I showed to the young rep. in question, hoping she'd take a lesson from it. See what I mean?'

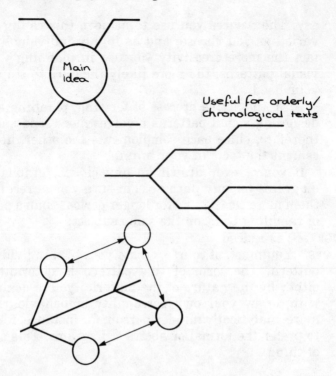

Useful for orderly/
chronological texts

[James shows the photocopies to Digby (see pp. 153, 154).]

DIGBY: 'I see how that pattern can stick in your mind for a longer time than written points one, two, and so on.'

JAMES: 'Apart from the visual impression it makes, the process of creating it involves you actively and so it registers and remains with you longer.

I can still recall, and this is going back many years, having to remember the main features of a particular camera in an advertisement brochure, in which I tried to retain the key points pictorially. I've always been completely unmechanically minded and knew nothing about cameras, so the terms were meaningless to me. My visual patterns would have been useless to anyone else, no doubt, but to me they made sense. For example. . .

COMPUTER STUDIES for GCSE

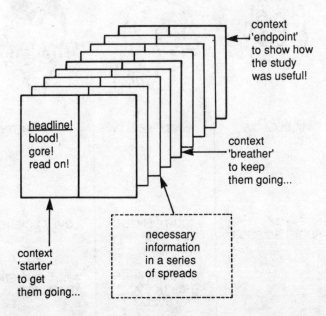

SUPPORTED BY:

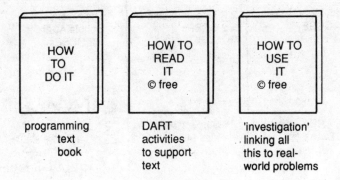

SCIENCE MODULE FOR MIXED ABILITIES OF PUPILS

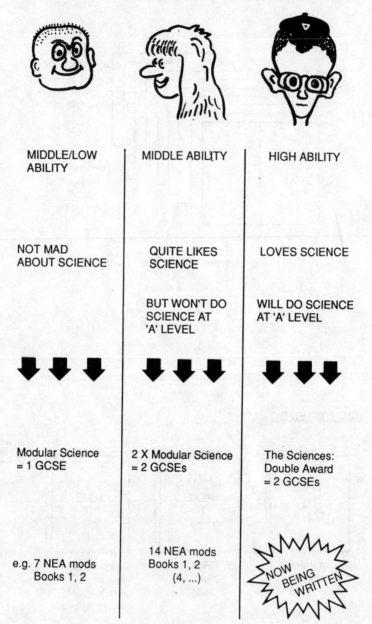

MIDDLE/LOW ABILITY	MIDDLE ABILITY	HIGH ABILITY
NOT MAD ABOUT SCIENCE	QUITE LIKES SCIENCE	LOVES SCIENCE
	BUT WON'T DO SCIENCE AT 'A' LEVEL	WILL DO SCIENCE AT 'A' LEVEL
Modular Science = 1 GCSE	2 X Modular Science = 2 GCSEs	The Sciences: Double Award = 2 GCSEs
e.g. 7 NEA mods Books 1, 2	14 NEA mods Books 1, 2 (4, ...)	NOW BEING WRITTEN

[grabbing a pen and paper and drawing, saying aloud the words as he labels the sketch]

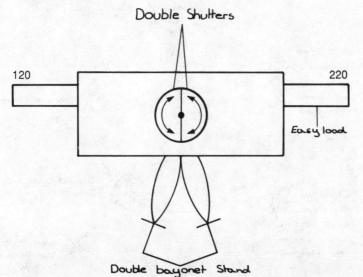

'and so on. God knows what double bayonet stand means or how it looks. It registered successfully for me, just as the two-way arrows remained in my mind as double shutters. I'm positive that if I'd just numbered and listed the main features in words, I'd never have retained them for twenty years.

The method is invaluable to salespeople for example, who have to retain features for all sorts of products.

A silly example, but one that brings the message home I think, is my wife's attempts to learn the words of Brahms' *Lullaby* to sing to Ben, our first grandchild. Feeling irritated that she kept getting certain of the images, phrases, in incorrect order, or forgetting them altogether, she scribbled within a minute, a visual diagram something like this.' (taking a pen and paper and sketching on it.)

[James draws the diagram (see p. 156).]

'She told me she never had to consciously learn the order of the images after having constructed it, thought it out. She just followed the visual in her

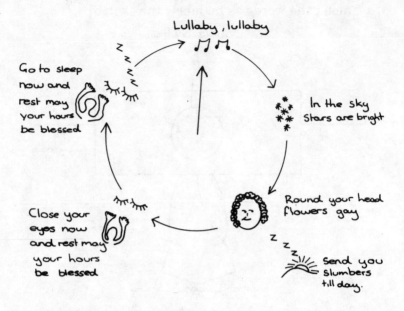

head as she sang and the words were firmly registered in her brain.'

DIGBY: 'Again, I see what you mean. Must you come to
these visual patterns via the questions and answers
you've asked in the first place, of the material you're
reading, I mean? Isn't there a short cut to your
patterns?'

JAMES: 'At times, yes. The question and answer is more
thorough for long pieces particularly, but I do
deviate from that method and go straight from
preview into my visual pattern for shorter pieces
with fewer main points to recall. They don't have to
be artistically creative, but if they're simple and
clear I can picture the diagram and repeat it
verbally. You might consider that a simple piece is
too easy to bother with a visual pattern, but drawing
up the plan fixes the facts in easily digestible form.

Of course, there are dozens of different types of
patterns you can choose. Develop your own to suit

you and the material you're attempting to commit to memory. Whichever you choose, they will help in the following ways:

(a) to clarify and summarize visually the relationships of all the facts you need to know and remember;

(b) to cement the information in your mind because you're actively ordering and arranging the information visually, and

(c) to provide a convenient summary when revising what you have learnt as part of the retention process.'

DIGBY: 'By the end of this stage, then, you feel the information should be more or less fixed in your head?'

JAMES: 'Almost. What now remains is for you to revise it immediately, go over it, to prevent the Ebbinghaus initial loss of retention occurring.'

DIGBY: 'The consolidation stage.'

JAMES: 'Correct. You revise what you've understood and formed patterns of, using as many of your senses as possible.'

DIGBY: 'What do you mean?'

JAMES: 'See the information, speak it and listen to it, write it, feel it if you can. Shut your eyes and visualize the patterns. The more you do with the information, the longer you'll retain it. For me, speaking it aloud is most valuable. There's no doubt that if you can openly talk about a subject you must know it. Going over it in your mind is open to abuse for you can deceive yourself by skipping over parts you're not too sure of and so on. So speak it aloud.

In addition you should write it down, firstly by reproducing the visual patterns which will test what you've recalled and what is missing, and in other ways such as writing a précis. Apart from checking what you know, the very act of writing helps lodge the information still more firmly in your brain. The motor and the visual senses reinforce each other.'

DIGBY: 'Is it advisable to tackle only one visual pattern at a time?'

JAMES: 'Yes, but people differ in their abilities and their

span of concentration, one cannot ignore that. On the whole it's better to tackle a limited section than feel swamped by too much. Again, the amount each individual can handle is a personal matter.

On the other hand, don't keep stopping to review too small a section. It must be a meaningful one, though I would rather err on the side of too short a selection than too long a one. As I've already mentioned I find it discouraging psychologically to have masses of print to master, and I'm sure I'm not alone in this. Rather set yourself shorter periods, in which you can prepare and recall a section methodically.

Research has shown that of groups of students spending the same time studying, those that spent half their time reading and half reviewing did better in their final recall.'

DIGBY: 'Come to think of it, I tend to tackle too long a section in one attempt, and I get harassed about not getting it all done.'

JAMES: 'Never underestimate the psychological aspect of any activity you undertake. In everything, and that includes studying, you should feel on top of things, confident, and this is difficult when you feel swamped.

But let's get on now. What's the next stage after your initial revising?'

DIGBY: 'Going over it at regular intervals, confirming you know it.'

JAMES: 'Yes. Of course, the shorter the intervals between these periods of revision the better and longer you'll retain the information.'

DIGBY: 'Perhaps at this point I should write down all the stages we've discussed. Let me see ... I'll work it out in a minute.'

JAMES: 'If you had a pattern, would that help? If I'd given a preview, showed you the steps we were to take, wouldn't that have made it easier to recall now?'

DIGBY: 'Probably.'

JAMES: 'I particularly chose not to do that, so you could see that it would have been clearer. The steps we covered were:

1 Purpose
2 Preview
3 Questions
4 Read for answers
5 Create visual patterns
6 Revise
7 Periodic review.

From these steps you could devise your own formula
of procedure, either by using the first letters of the
key words, or by changing the key words to suit a
formula which you'd find easy to remember, like
your MR Co Co. You could create a visual pattern,
it's entirely up to you how you retain the steps. But
first try them out, refine them for your own use, and
then devise a formula. The steps are there to help
you, to show you how to use the basic elements
involved in learning. Do with them what you will,
only think about them and try them out before
discarding them out of hand.'

DIGBY: 'One of the problems I have is finding a peaceful
undisturbed place in which to do all this methodical
study. It's so difficult to find a quiet place to work
at home, and at work it's impossible, so I tend to
move around.'

JAMES: 'Research suggests that we study best in one
specific place. We are creatures of habit and, in the
same way as to most people their own bed feels the
most comfortable, it's best to create a habitual place
of study if possible. A certain corner, table, chair,
becomes synonymous then with concentration and
work. And, of course, it's always better to study at
a table rather than on a settee or in bed. After all,
your eyes will already be half closed in that position.
A comfortable firm chair with good support for your
back is essential. Be comfortable, but not too
comfortable. It's only too easy to use reading as an
excuse for a doze. Reading should not be "an
ingenious device for avoiding thought", as Sir
George Helps claimed it to be for many individuals.
I think we're already agreed that reading must

involve thought of some sort if it's to be an activity of value.

Good lighting is important too. It should come from behind and onto the reading material. Too bright a light is trying on the eyes. As with any other activity, the more suitable the surroundings and the tools the better. Also, it's easier on the eyes to work with white paper against a lightly coloured desk than against a deeply contrasted one. So if you've a black desk for instance, it's not a bad idea to put down a large piece of paper or cloth to lessen the contrast between the book and background.

It's not a good idea to keep still in one position for hours on end. Move your body around every half hour or so. Your back, your neck, your eyes – look into the distance or close them – need a break. The odd minute now and then does wonders to send the blood flowing again and the muscles from settling in one position. This is all common sense, but worth remembering.'

DIGBY: 'These titbits of advice all help. Tell me, while we're on the subject of physical aspects of reading, are there any particular types of print that are easier or, conversely, more difficult to read?'

JAMES: 'There appears to be no difference between standard and bold print, no difference between most styles of typefaces in hardback and paperback – they're all much of a muchness. Shiny paper and print are less easy on the eyes, the glossies for instance, but comparatively little reading material you're likely to come across in daily life is of that calibre. The best is dull ink on dull white paper. Only typewritten material is apparently less comfortable on the eyes. Anything else you'd like to ask?'

DIGBY: 'Yes, there's one further important aspect of this whole question of studying and that's the collecting and storing of information. Basically we've discussed how to take information from one source and learn that only. My problem is how to collect information from a variety of sources. I take notes from each and then have to find relevant parts and put them together like a jigsaw.'

DIGBY: 'I know just what you mean, but don't worry, I intended coming to that. A systematic method of collecting and storing information is useful for everyone; the retired gentleman who wishes to collect and store gardening tips, or anyone with a hobby or interest.

Whatever the purpose, some organization is advisable to prevent sifting and sorting through sheets of paper to find specific points at a later stage. You should be able to check at a glance whether or not you've already made note of a particular point to avoid the trap of duplicating information. I can recall during my studies selecting masses of material and scrambling through the vast pile of notes, gleefully crossing out each page, or part of one, when I had safely deposited the required fact in its rightful place in my essay.

There are efficient ways of eliminating this haphazardness, whether you're preparing a short-term project such as gathering facts for a lecture, or long-term storing of information, perhaps with the prospect of writing a book one day. But even if you're only collecting and storing information for something less ambitious – a hobby perhaps – a systematic method makes sense. Let's look at how these systems work.

Suppose you're selected by your company to prepare a simple course on presentation skills for the executives under you. You're neither offered the opportunity to attend any courses, nor given any notes, but have to start from scratch and take all the information from books. For convenience, we'll use this same topic for both collating methods.

The first, simple and unsophisticated though it is, works admirably. I refer to it as the "column collation" method which is best suited to short-term projects.

Join together two sheets of A4 paper – lined if like me, you're unable to write straight without them. Divide them into columns, the width your own

162 Time manage your reading

choice. I generally have three columns per page. Take up your first choice of book – you've already previewed them. In this instance it would make sense to begin with a general book on presentations. At the top of the first column write "Title and author". As you go through the book and come across important sections relating to the topic head a new column, for example, "Preparation of presentation". Under that column note only the main relevant material you need, the key points, quotes. Don't copy whole extracts, be concise. You can note page numbers in specific points, but not too many or you'll have just as much material to go back to.

Moving on, as you come across other important facets of the subject, head a new column – "Use of voice", "Handling difficult audiences", and so on – and make the appropriate topic points you've come across.'

DIGBY: 'I can see how the column method forces you to be concise. You'll automatically feel restricted with limited writing space.'

JAMES: 'If you need more topic space, you can always add additional pages to your spreadsheet.

By the end of your first book, you'll have many columns written up. Rule across the entire sheet, and take up your next reference book. As you go through it, you'll already have noted some of the topics under the relevant column. You'll be able to see at a glance whether or not that point has been made, and won't waste time taking it down again in different words. If you find a new topic make another column for it, for example "Humour in presentations". With each new book or journal, go through the same process.'

DIGBY: 'Presumably you'll come across less and less information that needs noting.'

JAMES: 'Exactly. You might extract only one important point from an extraneous article or newspaper – make a note of it under the correct column.

By the time you've been through your complete bibliography you'll have all your information neatly classified, making it easy to set about constructing your presentation course.'

DIGBY: 'It sounds very efficient. It creates a sort of visual pattern making it easier to see and digest at a glance how many points you have on each topic, and also where you're short on information. This method would help in preparing for the XX project. I've already wasted time making haphazard notes.'

JAMES: 'I preferred to take you step by step through the reading skills as I feel they should be tackled, but it's not too late to use the method.'

DIGBY: 'What, go through it all again?'

JAMES: 'Just do the column collation on a smaller scale. Go through your notes and put those under columns for the different topics.'

DIGBY: 'I'll get onto that right away. It'll be a joy to reduce my heap to one single spreadsheet.'

JAMES: 'There are dozens of ways this method can be used for isolated projects such as writing speeches, local reports.'

DIGBY: 'I can see that. It's so simple, yet so practical. Schools should teach their pupils to use this method in preparing projects.'

JAMES: 'It would be invaluable. A project on any country could so easily be divided into columns, climate, industry, tourism and so on, rather than separate, muddling sheets.'

DIGBY: 'I shall pass this on to my kids.'

JAMES: 'With all this reading advice you'll turn them into top-class executives one day.'

DIGBY: 'I'll send them along to you for a job. But now I'm eager to hear your other method of collecting and collating facts.'

JAMES: 'That involves using the good old tickler box and index cards again, with a pack of alphabet cards to divide them. The method is essentially the same as the column collation, only you use separate cards for each topic.

Suppose, for instance, I start to collect information on all this "better reading" in order to write a book about it. I begin by reading a general book on the subject. As I come across each topic or unit that will become one in my book, I take an index card and write the topic as a heading on one side of it, such as anticipation, regression, studying, skimming and so on.

Under that heading, I list all the points I intend making in my book. I end up with a large wad of cards which I arrange alphabetically as I go along. The size of the cards and tickler box depends on the scale of the project, larger rather than too small of course.

As I come across further information, from other sources, relating to the book – a quotation, a new idea, an interesting example, well-put phrase and so on – I make a note of it and at the first opportunity transfer it to the relevant card.

Any subsequent idea that doesn't appear at that moment to belong under an existing topic, but which I feel may be useful, I file under the heading of Extras. At a later stage I'll probably find a home for it.'

DIGBY: 'As you say, this method seems an excellent approach for a long-term project.'

JAMES: 'Indeed. Not only can it be used at work, but any hobby or interest can find a safe, permanent and traceable home in a tickler box.

Tell me, have you ever been annoyed with yourself for not being able to recall where you came across a particular article or piece of information on a subject?'

DIGBY: 'Oh yes. I can kick myself sometimes when I want some information from a book and can't remember which one.'

JAMES: 'Well, wouldn't it be a good idea to note down the significant articles or parts of books under relevant topics and keep them in a tickler box? At a glance you could look up the subject, and it'll tell you where to find it. Your own library index, with all sorts of references, facts and figures. Saves time in the end when you desperately need some information. Most of us tend to be too lazy to bother with this sort of organization, think it's too time-consuming, but in the long run it pays off. All time management involves organization – as you go along.'

DIGBY: 'It's funny you should say that. Only last night I told my son that if he'd spend thirty seconds every evening putting his clothes away instead of dropping them on the floor, he wouldn't have to spend an hour sorting them out eventually, nor have to waste time each morning rummaging for what he needs.'

JAMES: 'Time management of our working life can invariably find an analogy in everyday life which underlines our inefficiency.

When you're classifying, there is sometimes the danger of forgetting under what topic you've recorded a particular item. If you want to recall where to find a wonderful collection of china cats, have you recorded them under "cats" or "china"? To be on the safe side remember to cross-reference, a card under cats and another under china.

I don't think I need to go any further into this, I'm sure you have the picture; but do remember to use the method. Once you start you'll find all sorts of uses for it. We all know about tickler boxes and filing cards, the question is do we make enough use of them? I doubt it.'

DIGBY: 'I'll certainly try them.'

JAMES: 'Good. It's been a long session, so we'll end here. Next week we'll have a final review of all we've been through and you can ask any questions that might come to mind as we go along.'

DIGBY: 'Many thanks, James. This has been a most informative session and I'll put it to good use. See you next week.'

Summary

Develop your own study formula based on the following steps.

Motivate yourself. Find reasons for studying each section you tackle.

Set yourself questions from the text taken from a preview for which you need the answers.

Read through the piece, writing the answers to the questions you've asked alongside them. Mark up the text itself, if possible.

Create visual recall patterns, either pictorial or diagrammatic, to register the information in your head.

Revise immediately and at periodic intervals. Write, speak, 'feel' the information.

Be systematic with the collecting and storing of information:

by using column collation for different aspects of the subject, and by using a tickler box and filing cards for the different aspects of the subject.

Executive action

Use the column collation method for the next presentation or speech for which you need to collect information.

See how many topics you can think up to store on index cards in a tickler box, both for work-related material and for outside use.

12 The complete reader

JAMES: 'Well, Digby, this is our last get-together over your reading. I trust you've sorted yourself out.'

DIGBY: 'I have and I'm most grateful to you James. You've quite revolutionized my whole approach to reading.'

JAMES: 'And would you say your approach is the heart of the matter?'

DIGBY: 'Yes, I've developed a systematic and skilful approach to it.'

JAMES: 'Let's look at some of the specifics you've achieved over the past two months. A review helps to consolidate and makes the picture clear. I'll start by asking you to recall how you felt before we had our first session. Can you sum up in a sentence what your general feeling towards your reading was at that point?'

DIGBY: 'Oh, unquestionably tense, unable to cope, always aware that I was reading far less of it than I should be and not getting the most I should from the reading I did do.'

JAMES: 'Did you feel this only with regard to work-related reading?'

DIGBY: 'No. I always felt there was a vast amount of valuable, entertaining, rewarding books I wanted to read but never did.'

JAMES: 'And now?'

DIGBY: 'Apart from coping so much better with what I need to read, I'm now enjoying my reading far more, particularly of more worthwhile and demanding books. I push myself into them and get wholly involved. I don't feel guilty if I skip some parts or don't understand others, I just get the most I can from what I do read. For instance, workwise, some of the articles you gave me as suggested reading for the XX project are in the *Harvard Business Review*, which I often find very difficult to comprehend. They don't flow for me. But after previewing, and then reading straight through those I know are important, without bothering with the complicated diagrams and details, I find I can understand an enormous amount.'

JAMES: 'Good. Would you say that an important aspect of your new skills is an increase in reading speed?'

DIGBY: 'Amazingly so. Last time I checked it, using your table to calculate speed, I was reading at more than double my original speed. With some simple relaxing paperbacks it was over 500 words per minute. Considering I started out at about 200 I'm more than happy.'

JAMES: 'So you must have overcome the barriers to speed?'

DIGBY: 'I certainly read for meaning, and having that in mind helps tremendously.'

JAMES: 'And can you now anticipate the general sense of what is to follow?'

DIGBY: 'Often. And I capitalize on it. I don't waste time reading what I already know, or know is coming.'

JAMES: 'Have you succeeded without regressing?'

DIGBY: 'Still do it occasionally I'm afraid, but I'm much better than I was. I'm aware when I have the odd lapse and pull myself up.'

JAMES: 'And subvocalizing?'

DIGBY: 'As you said, one can't eliminate it altogether, but since I've been going faster I'm definitely subvocalizing less. During some difficult sections or when I'm tired I find my tongue helping me to read, but if I force myself to keep it still I can feel myself hurrying along.

Of course reading vertically in newspapers and other narrow-columned articles certainly makes me go quicker. With my head moving down the page smoothly I can feel I'm getting faster. Also I've been able to read more than my usual set of newspapers, but I don't waste time reading what I've already learnt from the radio or TV news. I now take along a book as well as a newspaper to read on the train to work.'

JAMES: 'Would you say you're consciously aware of varying your speed to suit yourself?'

DIGBY: 'Oh yes. I've almost finished reading Arthur Miller's autobiography, *TimeBends*, and if I hadn't varied my speed over the six hundred odd pages I'm sure I'd never have read so much, nor enjoyed it so immensely. For instance, I'm not particularly interested in the Italian section so I hurdled across it, while still picking up the main events. If I'd tackled it in my old way, I'd have got bogged down there and used any old excuse to delay reading on. On the other hand his childhood fascinates me, and I read that more carefully, though still much faster than in the old days, and the atmosphere came alive for me. Then again his time with Marilyn Monroe is always interesting, but I've read quite a lot about it before and when I've found events I'm familiar with repeated in this book, I know them, so I've speeded up.'

JAMES: 'I'm delighted to hear you speak this way. But tell me, apart from these basic skills in reading, what specific new methods in your reading have you found most valuable?'

DIGBY: 'Previewing and skimming I think. I preview everything I read to a greater or lesser extent, even if only for a few seconds. It helps me to focus on it.'

JAMES: 'Is that the only way it helps?'

DIGBY: 'Oh no. I'm able to select books and articles far more accurately. Even in my leisure reading, I make far fewer mistakes in selecting a paperback from the bookshop. I never used to test the style, leaf through the way I do now. It pays to spend a little time on it.

Only yesterday I was looking through an article on "How to Write Articles" and I noticed a comment on plagiarism. It went on to explain that that was lifting other people's work and using it as your own. That told me at once that the article was a little too simple for me – I've read a lot on writing – so I didn't waste time reading it through. Previously I might have gone through the whole piece, perhaps only realizing halfway through that it was unlikely to give me much.

And of course previewing articles has been invaluable with the XX project. I've previewed dozens of articles and I just know I've selected the right ones. I tested it by reading through a few I'd discarded and they were definitely the correct ones to omit, a waste of time.'

JAMES: 'Do you feel the same way about skimming?'

DIGBY: 'Yes. As you said, it's an extended version of previewing and, again, I'm using it all the time. I've read articles I'd never have looked at in the old days because it was too time-consuming and laborious to read an entire article, especially if it was for idle curiosity or just a general interest in the subject.'

JAMES: 'Timewise you seem to be doing OK. How do you find your concentration and comprehension generally?'

DIGBY: 'Much improved.'

JAMES: 'And would you put that all down to a general improvement in your reading skills?'

DIGBY: 'Well to that, of course, but also because my approach is now an active one. I have a purpose. I know what I want. Just as my chess game is vastly better when I play with a good player – because the challenge is greater and, therefore, I concentrate more, so now that I have set goals I too concentrate more and therefore my comprehension is buoyed up. Also, with my increased speed, my attention doesn't flag as it used to do.'

JAMES: 'As far as concentration is concerned, when your mind wanders, that really involves great powers of concentration – your eyes work in one direction, your mind in another. The trick, of course, is to focus that attention on what your eyes are feeding you.'

DIGBY: 'As for comprehension, just feeling more confident in my approach to different reading materials seems to have had a positive effect on my comprehension, not to mention the streamlining of my general reading skills.'

JAMES: 'And are you questioning your reading, apart from setting your purpose?'

DIGBY: 'Yes, though I still have to think about that and at times I get lazy and don't bother. But I certainly see the value of doing so, asking specific questions in specific order. As I've said, I've learnt to be more discerning in my reading, selecting more carefully.'

JAMES: 'That's very important. As George Macaulay Trevelyan once said: "Education . . . has produced a vast population able to read but unable to distinguish what is worth reading". But go on, you were about to say. . .'

DIGBY: 'Oh yes! I'm more critical and that definitely helps my comprehension and concentration. I also find looking for the theme of a book is quite a challenge and puts it in perspective. It's a sort of summary of the book I have to think out for myself in a sentence or two.'

JAMES: 'Have you made any use of the studying that we spoke about last week?'

DIGBY: 'I've made a start. I've used the "one-ten" memory method often, for all sorts of things.'

JAMES: 'You make an admirable pupil, Digby. There's not much more for us to discuss. It seems to me you've gained some valuable insight into your reading and I'm sure you'll continue to be aware of all there is to it. Like all the other skills in life, you need to keep at it, constantly try to improve your performance.'

DIGBY: 'Certainly I could never go back to how I used to read. Now that my eyes have been opened to the vast depth and breadth of the subject, even if I never consciously thought about it again, I know the basic improvements will always be with me. For which, James, I'm extremely grateful. There's no doubt about it, reading is a vital aspect of our society.'

JAMES: 'No one could argue with that. It's not surprising that literacy is one of the criteria by which we assess the development of a country. Who can become truly educated without some form of reading?

It has been said that reading is to the mind what exercise is to the body – both are essential to today's well-rounded citizen. It's rather sad that so many people gain their information and entertainment from the television and other sources of amusement only, artificial props which they are able to use without any thinking involved. I hope that won't lead to an increase in the sentiments expressed by John Thorpe in Jane Austen's *Northanger Abbey*: "Oh Lord! not I; I never read much; I have something else to do."

I'll just read aloud a paragraph from this book, *How to Read a Book* by Mortimer J. Adler and Charles Van Doren: ". . . if we lack resources within ourselves, we cease to grow intellectually, morally, and spiritually. And when we cease to grow, we begin to die.

Reading well, which means reading actively, is thus not only good in itself, nor is it merely a means to advancement in our work or career. It also serves to keep our minds alive and growing."

But, ending on a more practical note, better reading skills will give you an advantage over others less skilled.'

DIGBY: 'Again, thank you James, for giving me a whole new outlook in such a vital field. I've no doubt that as a better reader I shall prove a better executive.'

Appendix: How to calculate your reading speed

1 Count the number of words in any five full lines of print in your book.
2 Divide this number by 5, to give you the average number of words per line.
3 Count the number of printed lines on a page (including lines with one word only, or a complete space).
4 Multiply '3' by '2', to give you the number of words per page. Round this off to the nearest 10 to give you a reasonable number to work with.

Time your reading

Mark the points at which you start and finish. Use a timer set at two or three minutes, or find someone to time you.

Assess the number of words read. For example, 2.5 pages at 340 words is 850 words read. (Take a rough estimate, to one-third or one-quarter of a page.)

Divide this by the number of minutes you read. For example, 850 words in three minutes is 283 words per minute.

NB. Don't worry about being precise. It's only a rough guide to test your progress.